EXPLOITING THE INTERNAL MARKET:
CO-OPERATION AND COMPETITION TOWARD 1992

Exploiting the internal market: co-operation and competition toward 1992

edited
by
P.J. Slot and M.H. van der Woude

Kluwer Law and Taxation Publishers
Deventer ● Antwerp
London ● Frankfurt ● Boston ● New York

Library of Congress Cataloging-in-Publication Data

Exploiting the internal market.

  1.   Restraint of trade – European Economic Community
countries.   2.   Antitrust law – European Economic
Community countries. I. Slot, Pieter J. II. Woude,
M.H. van der.
KJE6456.E96 1988   343.4′0723   88-13466
ISBN 90-6544-390-8   344.03723

D/1988/2664/91
ISBN 90 6544 390 8

Table of contents

Foreword

This book is the outcome of a Symposium organized at the University of Leiden on 1 July 1987 on the occasion of the 250th meeting of the 'Working group for European Competition Law' (Werkgroep Europees Kartelrecht). Some of the speeches delivered during the Symposium the theme of which was 'Co-operation and Competition', have been rewritten as articles for this publication.

The working group was founded in 1958. It meets once a month at the University of Leiden to discuss informally recent developments in EEC Competition Law. Its members are all professionally concerned with this area of law. Their professions are, however, very diverse; academics, practising lawyers, in-house counsel of multinaltional companies, magistrates, officials from the Commission of the European Communities and the Ministry of Economic Affairs in The Hague. This diversity and the informal character of the meetings allow for a vivid discussion and a mutual exchange of information. We hope that this diversity is also reflected in this book.

The manuscript has been finalized in January 1988. Subsequent developments have not been taken into account.

Finally, we would like to express our gratitude to Mr A. Lewis for his revision of the English texts, to Ms H. Sevenster for her organizational assistance and to Ms E. Cramer for her secretarial support.

P.J. Slot   *M.H. van der Woude*

List of contributors

W. Alexander is a member of the Bar of The Hague and partner of Barents, Gasille & Mout.

M. van Empel is a member of the Bar of Amsterdam and partner of Stibbe & Blaisse. He is also professor of Economic Law at the University of Amsterdam.

B. van der Esch is special Counsel to De Brauw and Westbroek in The Hague and former senior legal counsellor of the EC Commission.

H.W. de Jong is professor in the Faculty of Economics of the University of Amsterdam.

R.H. Lauwaars is professor of the Law of International Organizations at the University of Amsterdam.

P.J. Slot is professor of Economic Law at the University of Leiden.

J.F. Verstrynge is a member of the cabinet of EC Commissioner Sutherland responsible for competition policy.

R.D. Visser, Legal Dept. Shell International Petroleum Maatschappij, The Hague.

H.W. Witlox is a former counsellor of the EC Commission's Directorate General IV.

M.H. van der Woude is an official of the EC Commission's Directorate-General IV.

Introduction

Hardly a day goes by without reading or hearing about 1992. This date refers to Article 8A of the EEC Treaty as amended by the European Single Act. The Article foresees the establishment of an 'internal market' before 31 December of that year. An internal market signifies a single area without internal borders in which free circulation of goods, persons, services and capital is guaranteed according to the provisions of the EEC Treaty. These provisions have been amended or supplemented by the European Single Act. In the common declaration of the Member States on Article 8A of the Act, reference is made to the Commission's White Paper as a programme of measures for the completion of the internal market.[1]

It should be noted that the White Paper only concerns free circulation. Neither the Single Act nor the White Paper foresees any specific measures in the field of competition policy. This omission may at first sight appear somewhat surprising since competition policy directly concerns European enterprises. Enterprises are supposed to derive the greatest benefit from the establishment of a true internal market. They can, however, also undermine its operation and effectiveness through restrictive behaviour. Although it does not contain any specific measures concerning competition policy, the White Paper explicitly recognizes the importance of competition rules in the framework of the internal market. Paragraph 19 of the White Paper states that any action which promotes free circulation should necessarily be accompanied by a strengthening of the Commission's control of compliance by undertakings and Member States with the competition rules. A strong and coherent competition policy should above all ensure that restrictive practices do not lead to a segmentation of the internal market.

Apart from the objective of integration which has guided the Commission's competition policy since the early 1960's, competition should, of course, also promote the optimal allocation of resources. The pursuit of both objectives, integration and optimal allocation, does not, however, preclude co-operation between companies, especially where co-operation contributes to an increase in efficiency and competiveness of European industry.

To establish and operate a strong and coherent internal market it is essential to facilitate transfer of technology, research and development activities, industrial restructuring and even market integration. They may well

---

[1] COM (A5) 310 final.

require entrepreneurial co-operation. It is therefore necessary that the Community's competition rules clearly define the scope of co-operation.

The purpose of this book is to show that the Community's competition policy already provides a complete and mature set of rules adapted to the needs of 1992, albeit with some exceptions such as, for example, comprehensive and *a priori* merger control. The EEC competition policy has been developed since the entry into force of the EEC Treaty and has determined the extent to which co-operation between firms may take place. The European Single Act did not foresee any amendment of the Treaty's competition rules. This may be taken as an indication of the mature character of this policy.

The book illustrates and examines this aspect in the light of 1992 by dealing with the following issues:

1. What are the main characteristics and tendencies of the present system of competition rules?
2. What should be the criteria for the assessment of co-operation between companies and co-operation within companies?
3. More specifically, what are the legal constructions permitting such co-operation?

It should be noted in this respect that the book does not attempt to discuss these issues exhaustively. Its articles focus on specific topics which are indicative of the present and future developments in EEC competition law.

To begin with, there are three contributions focussing upon the first issue. *Verstrynge* describes the nature of the system of EEC competition rules. In the process of completing a truly single market the emphasis of competition policy will shift from the objective of market integration to the achievement of optimal resource allocation within that market. In this respect the Commssion will give greater attention to economic analysis. Its role will become more policy-oriented. It will continue to work on the completion of an elaborate legislative programme and the issue of 'trendsetting' individual decisions. This programme and these decisions will further enhance a decentralized enforcement by the national courts.

Van Empel questions whether these developments amount to a system of European competition rules. He doubts whether competition is the prime organizational principle behind the European rules concerning private enterprises and whether the enforcement of competition rules can really be effective. Is the Commission extending its powers under Article 85(1) without also providing for the means for an effective implementation?

The third article by *Slot* gives a concrete illustration of the issues raised by the preceding authors. For a long time sea transport, like air transport,[2]

---

[2] Regulation 3975/87 (OJ L 374/1 1987) and Regulation 3976/87 (OJ L 374/9 1987) provide for procedural rules and a block-exemption in this sector.

appeared to fall outside the scope of the system of competiton rules. At present Regulation 4056/86[3] provides far an enforcement procedure for competition in the shipping sector. It simultaneously contains a block-exemption for liner conferences and for agreements between liner-companies and shippers. It also provides for an interesting mechanism to resolve jurisdiction conflicts with third countries. Regulation 4056/86 completes the system but how effective will its implementation be?

The two articles which follow tackle the second of the aforementioned issues. *De Jong* points out that the EEC Treaty relies on the competitive process as the instrument for structuring the economy. This process appears not only to possess an internal dynamism but if also has structural impacts. Such 'restructuring' can either lead to concentrations or to co-operation between the firms involved. It is the aim of EEC competition policy to supervise this delicate process. It does not preclude restructuring operations through concentration and co-operation so long as they do not impair the competitive process. Co-operation can, therefore, be permitted if its final results are procompetitive.

Witlox's contribution examines restructuring operations through merger-like behaviour which have – to a certain extent – already taken place. Large transnational companies and their subsidiaries are normally well-established throughout the Common Market. Their distribution-systems and pricing policies may, however, endanger the operation and even the completion of the internal market. Witlox, therefore, advocates a more effective control of co-operation between companies belonging to a transnational group.

The final issue, the legal construction permitting co-operation, is the subject of the following three articles. As indicated by De Jong, the competitive process may lead to restructuring. The completion of an internal market before or after 1992 will undoubtedly entail such restructuring through co-operation or concentration. In this context joint ventures may play a useful role.

Van der Esch reviews this particular form of co-operation. Joint ventures should be assessed positively when they ultimately lead to increased competition. It is, however, very difficult to give specific criteria in this respect. Van der Esch examines the Commission's practice concerning joint ventures under Article 85(1) to clarify their impact. In his view, joint ventures should be treated as forms of co-operation under Article 85(1) and not be classified as mergers.

This problem of classification directly affects the scope of the system of EEC competition rules. It also arises in Lauwaars' article on industrial restructuring operations. These operations often take the form of joint ventures. After describing the Commission's practice in this field, *Lauwaars* concludes that such operations should be assessed under a new merger

[3] OJ L 378/4 1987.

control regulation. Such a regulation has not yet been adopted by the Council.

Alexander's article focuses on licensing as form of co-operation which generates fewer problems of classification. Alexander proposes that licensing operations should be assessed by balancing the restrictions relating to the licensed technology against the competition between this technology and comparable technologies. Accordingly, he examines the Commission's licensing policy.

Finally, *Visser's* article takes us beyond the limits of Community competition policy. It demonstrates how an almost completely integrated European natural gas market has already been established. The role of the European authorities and of European law has been relatively insignificant in this context. The creation of this market has resulted from the interaction of national authorities, public undertakings and private enterprises.

P.J. Slot/M.H. van der Woude

I. The system of EEC competition rules

JEAN-FRANÇOIS VERSTRYNGE[1]

1. Introduction

The system of antitrust rules embodied in the EEC Treaty has now been in existence for about 30 years since 1958 when that Treaty came into force.

Starting form the basic rules of the Treaty – Articles 85 and 86, and to a lesser extent Article 90 – a complete system of rules and powers has been constructed and operated. This system now includes about half a dozen regulations of the Council of Ministers. More than a dozen regulations of the European Commission, as well as about a dozen general notices (which could be compared to guidelines) from the same Commission. It has also produced about 150 judgments of the European Court of Justice in Luxemburg, more than 250 individual decisions of the Commission, as well as an increasing number of judgments from national courts of the Member States of the EEC, including some rendered by the various national supreme courts.

Looking back at the whole system, it can be stated that the system has, with a few exceptions, touched upon all important or relevant problems connected with the field of antitrust. If one compares it, for instance, with the system which has now existed for almost a century in the United States, it is possible to conclude that most problems related to the antitrust field which arose in the US have now also, in one way or another, been dealt with by the system of competition rules of the EEC Treaty.

There remain, however, a few lacunas in the system, such as the missing regulation of the Council of Ministers regarding the introduction of a control on concentrations and mergers. In its resolution on the fifteenth competition report, the European Parliament has advised the Comission to withdraw its proposal for such a regulation and to look for alternative means of merger control.[2]

---

[1] Member, Cabinet of Commissioner Sutherland, Commission of the European Communities, Brussels.
  The opinions expressed in this paper reflects only the opinions of the author.
[2] The application of Article 85(1) and (3) could offer such an alternative for the control of certain types of mergers. A related Commission notice could then clarify the difficulties of such a possible application. In this way this structural gap might be partially filled up.

1

Another lacuna is to be found in the air transport sector. Political difficulties between Spain and Great Britain concerning the souvereignity of Gibraltar prevented the adoption of the Commission proposals for two Council regulations on the application of Article 85 and 86 on air transport.[3]

These limited defects in the system of competition rules cannot hinder the conclusion that this system has now reached after 30 years a large degree of maturity. In almost all areas of economic activity, enterprises have to take it into account.

The purpose of this contribution is to offer some updated reflexions on the current competition policy issues in the EEC at this particular moment of time when the system has entered, so to say, its second generation. The impact of these tendencies on the commercial behaviour of enterprises will be discussed, as well as the impact on the possibilities for co-operation between enterprises. In section 2 this paper will highlight some of the present tendencies in the competition policy of the European Communities. The impact of these developments on co-operation between enterprises will be discussed in section 3.

2. Present tendencies

I believe that the present tendencies in the competition policy of the European Communities can be related to the following four main directions in which the system is developing:

a) a shift of emphasis between the different objectives of the system with increased emphasis on the antitrust objectives relating to the conduct of a policy;

b) a move to take economic reality into account to a larger extent than before;

c) a still growing concern with 'legal security' and

d) a tendency to decentralize the enforcement towards national courts.

These tendencies will be examined and commented on one by one.

A. A shift of emphasis between the two objectives

As is generally known, EEC competition policy has two main objectives.

The *first* one is principally related to market integration or market unification. This objective originates from a basic idea which is already present in

---

[3] In the meantime this lacuna has been remedied by the adoption of the regulations decided by the Council of Ministers of the twelve Member States in December 1987.

the Spaak Report of 1956 (preparing the Messina Conference which gave rise to the adoption of the EEC Treaty). This objective is that a Treaty concerning economic integration which imposes on the Member States rules intended to allow free operation of economic forces through free movement of goods, services, persons and capital, cannot at the same time allow private economic operators to have the power to defeat the free play of these forces by market allocation conspiracies or abuse of dominant market power. Hence the necessity to include in the EEC Treaty a system of antitrust rules aimed at prohibiting such practices and at promoting market integration or unification. This objective remains of a paramount importance considering the present program to complete the internal market by 1992.

The first objective has been repeatedly emphasized by the European Court of Justice over the years, starting with the *Grundig-Consten* case in 1966:

> 'Finally an agreement between producer and distributor which might tend to restore the national divisions in trade between Member States might be such as to frustrate the most fundamental objectives of the Community. *The Treaty, whose preamble and content aim at abolishing the barriers between States, and which in several provisions gives evidence of a stern attitude with regard to their reappearance, could not allow undertakings to reconstruct such barriers. Article 85(1) is designed to pursue this aim*, even in the case of agreements between undertakings placed at different levels in the economic process.'[4]

The second objective of competition policy has more to do with the functioning of competition itself on the market place. It relates also more to the operation of economic policy. The second objective – which is also present in the EEC Treaty – was first highlighted by the European Court in the *Walt-Wilhelm* case in 1969:

> 'Any other solution would be incompatible with the objectives of the Treaty and the character of its rules on competition. Article 85 of the EEC Treaty applies to all the undertakings in the Community whose conduct it governs either by prohibitions or by means of exemptions, granted – subject to conditions which it specifies – in favour of agreements which contribute to improving the production or distribution of goods or to promoting technical or economic progress. While the Treaty's primary object is to eliminate by this means the obstacles to the free movement of goods within the common market and to confirm and safeguard the unity of that market, it also permits the Community authorities to carry out certain positive, though indirect, action with a

---

[4] *Consten and Grundig v. Commissions*, cases 56 & 58/64, 13 July 1966, ECR 1966, page 299.

view to promoting a harmonious development of economic activities within the whole Community, in accordance with Article 2 of the Treaty.'[5]

Behind the application of EEC competition rules, and in particular behind the application of Article 85(3), lies in fact a *policy-making power*. It can therefore be said that the European Commission conducts a real competition *policy* and does not limit its role to the mere enforcment of legal rules as a prosecution authority would do, with decisions whether to prosecute or not given violations. This *competition policy* can then be influenced by the general economic policy (including industrial policy), which the European Commission is conducting in the framework of the EEC Treaty.

The shift of emphasis on the second objective is occurring slowly but constantly. It can be noticed particularly in the most recent development and it has already been publicly commented on by the European Commission in the introduction to its Thirteenth Report on Competition Policy:

'It was this aim which also guided the work of the Commission in 1983, in both the control of restrictive practices and of State aids. Thus the Commission reaffirmed the principles already stated in the Twelfth Report that in a market economic system such as that of the Community, it is essential to preserve the stimulus of fair and effective competition in order that the economy can reap the benefits of free trade. The decisions the Commission took hence reflected a continuing determinating to rigorously enforce the competition rules, but also a desire to encourage industrial restructuring, to improve the competitiveness of European industry, to promote research and development and innovation, and to accelerate the progress towards a single Community market.

As this shows, the Commission's work of administering competition policy cannot be encapsulated by the sole objective of removing distortions caused by anticompetitive practices of State aids which are liable to interfere with inter-State trade. Competition policy also contributes to improving the allocation of resources and raising the competitiveness of Community industry, and thanks to this greater competitiveness, secured largely by encouragement of research and development, to enabling the Community at length to overcome the economic problems now facing it and in particular to combat structural unemployment. In this way, competition policy can play its part, with other Community policies, in securing a lasting economic recovery.'[6]

---

[5] *Wilhelm v. Bundeskartellamt*, Case 19/68, 13 February 1969, ECR 1969, page 1.
[6] *Commission Thirteenth Report on Competition Policy II* (1984).

Of course, both objectives remain present in the system and continue to be pursued. The European Commission does not in any way appear to intend to abandon the pursue of the first objective in favour of the second one. In fact, it seems that the shift lies in giving an increased emphasis to this second objective in comparison to the past.

The main reasons for this shift are most probably related not only to the depth and length of the ongoing economic difficulties, but also to the fact that the EEC system has reached adulthood in its development.

Examples of decisions of the European Commission in this respect are numerous. One could pinpoint the decision under Article 85(3) concerning the crisis cartel in the synthetic fibre industry,[7] the action relating to the *IBM* case under Article 86,[8] or the change of orientation concerning territorial protection in the group exemption on patent licensing,[9] as being clear examples of this tendency.

Very important consequences flow from the direction the system has taken, with respect to both the substantive field of application of the system and to the organization of the system itself.

As far as the *substance* is concerned, the development which has occurred means that competition policy is not managed in a sort of vacuum (as a body of law finding its *raison d'être* in and of itself), but in relation to the other policies of the EEC Treaty conducted by the European Commission. This will also mean that the application of this competition policy is to be managed with some coherent economic thinking behind it. It further means that this application can be influenced by other policies such as, but not limited to, industrial or agricultural policy, research policy, transport policy, environmental policy, consumer protection policy, etc. In this context a just equilibrium between free competition und co-operation between enterprises has to be found.

The Court of Justice already gave an indication in its *Metro* ruling of 1979 that the competences of the Commission under para. 3 of Article 85 show that the maintenance of *workable competition* can be reconciled with the safeguarding of policy objectives of a different nature.[10] Moreover, the action of the Commission itself in the *IBM* case shows that not only Article 85(3), but also Article 86 opens policy perspectives which go beyond the mere antitrust objective. The IBM settlement has promoted, apart from free competition in the computer market, further standardization and development of this market.

As far as *organization* is concerned, these developments assume and necessitate that competition policy be conducted by a single decision-making center, which is the European Commission. Any policy risks becoming

---

[7] Synthetic Fibres, OJ L 207/17 (2 August 1984).
[8] Commission Press Release, IP(84) 290 (2 August 1984).
[9] Commission Regulation No. 2349/84, OJ L 219/15 (16 August 1984).
[10] Case 26/76, *Metro v. Commission*, 25 October 1977, ECR 1977, page 1875.

meaningless and incoherent if several independent decision-making bodies conduct it. From an organisational point of view, it is therefore necessary that the present distribution of powers over Community competition policy remains unchanged.

This shift in emphasis which, in my opinion, is irreversible, will in the second generation of EEC competition policy be accentuated and completed by the emergence of both the overall and sectoral thinking of the European Commission in relation to economic and industrial organization. It is therefore to be expected that the power to grant group exemptions will become one of the major instruments by which the European Commission steers its competition policy in coordination with the other policies of the European Communities. Competition policy thus becomes part of the overall economic policy the Commission is pursuing. This is not surprising since the European Court already indicated in one of its judgments in 1969 that a link exists between the economic objectives of Article 2 of the Treaty and the competition rules, and in particular with Article 85(3).[11]

Since 1985 this way of conducting competition policy has even been reinforced by the actions of Commissioner Sutherland, in particular in relation to joint ventures, know-how licences and franchising.

B.   Taking greater account of economic reality

Another tendency in the second generation of the EEC competition policy will definitely be that the operation of this policy will take economic reality more and more into consideration.

The European Court of Justice opened the way for this already in 1966 and 1967 in two of its earliest judgments. The first one was given in the *Société Technique Minière/Maschinenbau Ulm* case and the second one in the *Brasserie de Haecht I* case.[12] These rulings meant that the antitrust provisions of the EEC Treaty are based on an economic assessment of the behaviour under scrutiny and that these provisions therefore cannot be interpreted as introducing any kind of advance judgment with regard to a category of behaviour determined by its legal nature. To constitute an infringement, such behaviour has therefore to be considered in the entire economic and legal context in which it takes place.

Apart from the fact that these rulings de facto excluded the appearance of 'per se' offences in EEC antitrust law, they have had some far-reaching consequences for the orientation of EEC competition policy, which can be

---

[11] Speech of Commissioner Andriessen of 23 January 1984 to the International Bar Association meeting in Brussels.

[12] Case 56/65, *LTM/MBU*, 30 June 1966, ECR 1966, page 235. Case 23/67, *Brasserie de Haecht v. Wilkin & Janssen*, 12 December 1967, ECR 1967, page 525.

witnessed even today. Indeed, they resulted in an increasing trend of taking into account economic reality to a larger extent. This trend exists both in the legislative part of the Commission's activity, as well as in the examination of individual cases.

First, on the *legislative* side, the Commission could start adopting regulations which are not applicable to the whole economy, but which are industrially or sectorally tailored. The first example of such a tendency lies in Regulation 1984/83 which contains specific provisions for beer supply agreements and for service station agreements.[13] The Commission has also adopted a group exemption regulation concerning motor vehicle distribution and servicing agreements.[14] Regulation 4056/86 on the application of Articles 85 and 86 to maritime transport offers another example of this sectoral policy approach.[15] At this point, mention should also be made of the greenbook on telecommunications.[16] This book, in which the Commision indicates which telecom policy it intends to follow, illustrates both its sectoral approach and its coherent economic thinking. In this particular sector of the economy competition objectives have to be weighted against other policy objectives. The work programme to be put in motion following this greenbook might very well include directives or decisions of the Commission based on Article 90(3).

Thus clearly the application of EEC antitrust system on the legislative side moves in the direction of closer ties with underlying economic reality. This tendency does not result necessarily in more regulated industries; it can also result in more competitive freedom. Adopting a regulation to make antitrust rules applicable can indeed correspond to deregulation.

The same tendency can also be seen in the *examination of individual cases*. The reasons and recitals of individual decisions, which according to Article 190 of the EEC Treaty must be given by the Commission, become more and more detailed and include more and more economic reasoning as time goes by. Over the years the European Court of Justice has become increasingly strict with the Commission in this respect. In the *United Brands* case[17] the part of the Commission's decision concerning unfair prices was annulled because the Commission had not rebutted United Brand's arguments with sufficient economic analyses.[18] Thereafter, two individual decisions of the Commission (in the *Michelin*[19] and *Hasselblad* cases[20] were

---

[13] OJ L 173/5 (30 June 1983), as amended OJ L 281/24 (13 October 1983).
[14] OJ L 15/16 (18 January 1985).
[15] OJ L 378/4 (12 December 1986).
[16] COM 87 (290) final.
[17] Case 27/76, *United Brands v. Commission,* 14 February 1978, ECR 1970, page 207.
[18] See ECR 1978 at page 235–68.
[19] *Bandengroothandel Friescheburg BV v NV Nederlandse Banden Industrie Michelin,* OJ L 353/33 (12 December 1981).
[20] *Hasselblad,* OJ L 161/18 (12 June 1982).

again annulled in part, either because the Commission was unable to demonstrate the alleged infringements with sufficient facts[21] or because it misinterpreted the economic meaning of the factual evidence.[22]

Thus the reasoning of the Commission in individual cases is scrutinized by the European Court with increasing severity. This encourages the Commission to give more detailed reasons and to rely more closely on the factual economic reality and on economic reasoning in its individual decisions.

The reasoning relied upon by the Commission in individual cases sometimes includes even a detailed analysis of the whole sector, even though only a few companies are directly concerned in a given case. An example of this can be seen in the action of the Commission in the petrochemical sector. Several individual cases were examined in an industry-wide context.[23] Hence decisions like *ICI/BP*,[24] and *Irish Bank's Standing Committee*[25] contain detailed sectorial analyses.

The fact that the Commission takes greater account of economic reality does not mean that it adheres to the use of what is called the 'Rule of Reason' under Article 85(1). The adherents of the use of such a concept complain that the Commission takes an inflexible approach in the application of Article 85(1), without conducting sufficient economic analyses with respect to the reasonableness of restrictions under that provision. An additional test of reasonableness should, according to them, be introduced into that provision, even when all the constitutive elements of an infringement of Article 85(1) are present. This concept cannot be accepted.

First, if all the authorities competent for the application of EEC competition rules modulated the prohibition of Article 85(1) by what they consider to be reasonable, the consequence would be legal insecurity through lack of uniformity and renationalisation of competition policy in particular through the undermining of the central policy making power of the Commission under Article 85(3).

Second, when examining behaviour under the prohibition of Article 85(1), the Commission, as already said above, considers that behaviour in its entire economic and legal context. The construction and wording of Article 85 clearly show that when additional flexibility is desirable, Article 85(3) allows for exemption from the prohibition of paragraph 1. It is under the operation of Article 85(3) that the Commission can be said to apply an approach which resembles the American 'Rule of Reason'.

Another aspect of this tendency to take greater account of economic reality can be witnessed in the efforts of the Commission to apply competi-

---

[21] Case 322/81, *NV Nederlandse Banden Industrie v. Commission*, 9 November 1983, ECR 1983, page 346.
[22] Case 86/82, *Hasselblad, (GB), Ltd. v. Commission*, 21 February 1984, ECR 1984, page 883.
[23] *See Commission Thirteenth Report on Competition Policy*, 56–61 (1984).
[24] OJ L 212/1 (8 August 1984).
[25] OJ L 295/28 (18 October 1986).

tion policy in all sectors of the economy, and in particular in the service sectors. Since 1985 Commissioner Sutherland has initiated or pursued several actions aimed at the transport sector (air and sea), at the financial sector (banking, insurance, commodity markets), at the telecommunications sector and at the cultural sector.

The tendency to take greater account of economic reality is even reflected in the way the relevant services of the Commission are organised. Recently the Directorate General for Competition was reorganised in several ways. One of the elements of this reorganisation concerns the creation of more sectoral divisions inside Directorate B, C and D of DG IV.

This growing concern with economic reality is a sure sign of maturity of the system. After a period during which the basic principles of this system (which apply necessarily to the whole economy) have been established, it is now possible to move to more detailed economic analysis, more sectorally tailored. In my opinion this tendency will not be reversed.

C. Growing concern for 'legal security'

This requirement of 'legal security' (i.e. certainty as to one's legal position in individual cases) has always been an important element in the application of the competition rules of the EEC Treaty. Since Articles 85 and 86 were drafted in rather general terms, some uncertainty remained when they had to be applied to a wide range of very difficult factual situations. The language of Article 85(3) in particular is drafted in very broad terms, rendering some economic appreciation necessary.

Moreover, agreements falling under Article 85(2) become automatically void. The Court of Justice ruled that this invalidity is of an absolute nature (*Brasserie de Haecht II* case)[26] and is even retroactive (*Béguelin* case).[27]

In the early years, the question of the provisional validity of agreements lay at the center of the discussions as a possible way of reconciling the stringency of the directly applicable provisions of Articles 85(1) and 85(3). The Commission in the first instance had attempted to deal with this problem by issuing several notices in the Official Journal of the European Communities, by building up a whole range of test cases to clarify to what extent the rules concerned are applicable, and by publishing a yearly report on competition policy since 1970.

The fact remains, however, that such notices – which could be compared to guidelines – or indeed the yearly report, have no binding force under Article 189 of the EEC Treaty, although they are sometimes relied upon by

---

[26] Case 48/72, *Brasserie de Haecht v. Wilkin & Janssen*, 6 March 1973, ECR 1973, page 77.
[27] Case 22/71, *Béguelin Import v. G.L. Import-Export*, 25 November, 1971 ECR 1971, page 949.

the Commission in procedures before the Court in Luxemburg. Moreover, the number of individual decisions taken each year has remained limited.

Even after these positive actions of the Commission (and even if the case law of the Court and the administrative practice of the Commission has developed considerably), the need for legal security remained. This need can even be said to increase over time, since it becomes less and less acceptable to leave certain areas of the system unclarified.

It is partly in response to this situation that the Commission decided to speed up and enlarge the legislative activity related to this system and, in particular, group exemptions. Indeed, group exemptions based on Article 85(3) and on implementing an area of absolute legal protection. Agreements covered by group exemptions cannot be declared void, cannot give rise to fines and are not subject to actions for damages in national courts.

The system has therefore moved to codify the administrative practice of individual decisions and past notices (guidelines) of the Commission into regulations, granting group exemptions under Article 85(3). In 1983 two such regulations replaced[28] – and modified or completed – Regulation 67/67.[29] In 1984 an entirely new group exemption for patent licences was enacted.[30] In 1985 three further group exemptions were adopted by the Commission. Regulation 123/85[31] concerning distribution agreements in the motor vehicle sector. Regulation 417/85 enlarging former Regulation 3604/82 on specialisation agreements[32] and Regulation 418/85 on R & D cooperation.[33]

In 1986 the Council adopted Regulation 4056/86 which provides not only for the procedural rules necessary for the application of Articles 85 and 86 to maritime transport,[34] but also for a group exemption for certain maritime conferences. (At the end of 1987 the Council adopted a regulation empowering the Commission to grant group exemptions in the air transport sector.) In addition, two more group exemption regulations could be adopted by the Commission in 1988, one on know-how licensing agreements and another on franchising.[35]

The completion of this legislative programme has had and will continue to have the effect of reducing considerably the degree of legal uncertainty that remains in the system. It is already clear that the adoption of group exemptions will be, if not the most important, at least one of the most important

---

[28] Commission Regulation No. 1983/83, OJ L 173/1 (30 June 1983). Commission Regulation No. 1984/83, OJ L 173/5 (30 June 1983).

[29] Commission Regulation No. 67/67, OJ 57/849 (25 March 1967).

[30] Commission Regulation No. 2349/84, OJ L 219/15 (16 August 1984).

[31] OJ L 15/16 (18 January 1985).

[32] OJ L 53/1 (22 February 1985).

[33] OJ L 53/5 (22 February 1985).

[34] OJ L 378/9 (12 December 1986).

[35] Draft regulation know-how licensing agreements, OJ C214/2 (12 August 1987): Draft Regulation franchising agreements OJ C229/3 (27 August 1987).

future activities of the Comission in this field. Several other group exemptions could be envisaged; for example, for copyright licences or in the insurance sector.

Whatever the future developments will be, the number of group exemptions will only be enlarged and not reduced and such initiatives to respond to the need for legal security will remain part of the system.

D. Decentralisation of the enforcement towards national courts

Substantial enforcement powers were given by the EEC Treaty and by Regulation 17/62 to the European Commission and in particular, by Articles 3, 9 and 15 of this regulation.[36] The largest part of the enforcement burden has up to now rested on the Commission. The number of cases in which the national courts applied Articles 85 or 86 remained rather limited even if it is at present increasing. Indeed, in the early years antitrust rules were new for most Member States and the national courts were unaccustomed to them.

However, the European court of Justice opened the way to a more decentralised enforcement of these rules by national courts by declaring Articles 85(1) and 86 directly applicable by national courts in its BRT/SABAM judgment in 1973.[37] It further declared Article 85(2) directly applicable in several cases.

The present increase in the number of group exemptions will further enlarge this decentralisation towards national courts. Indeed, under Article 189 of the EEC Treaty regulations, whether of the Council or of the Commission, are directly applicable by nature. Thus any group exemption regulation under Article 85(3) can also be directly applied by national courts (always subject of course to the reference procedure of Article 177). For that part of the substantive matter covered by a group exemption regulation, the enforcement of the system is in this way automatically decentralized towards the national courts.

This tendency to decentralise the enforcement of the system towards national courts can also be seen in other ways. The Commission has recently recognized that it is desirable that judicial enforcement of Articles 85 and 86 should include the award of single (not treble) damages to injured parties in order to render this part of Community law more effective.[38]

---

[36] Council Regulations No. 17/62, OJ C 13/204 (20 April 1962).

[37] Case 127/73, *Belgische Radio en Televisie v. SABAM,* 30 January 1974, ECR 1974, page 51, and 27 March 1974, ECR 1974, page 313.

[38] Commission Answer to Parl. Qu. No. 1935/83, OJ C 144/14 (30 May, 1984), *See* generally Temple Lang, EEC Competition Actions in Member States' Courts – Claims for Damages and Injunctions for Breach of Community Antitrust Law, in 1983 Fordham Corp. L. Inst. 219 (B. Hawk ed. 1984).

The principle that damages should be awarded for violations of EEC antitrust rules has already been recognized by several of the national supreme courts of the Member States. The German Bundesgerichtshof accepted the principle in the *BMW* case at the end of 1979.[39] Since then it has also been accepted by the French Cour de Cassation in 1982[40] and by the House of Lords in the *Milk Marketing Board* case in 1983.[41]

The adoption of measures ensuring that this principle will be a more effective part of Community competition law and will be increasingly applied by national courts also has the effect of decentralizing the enforcement of these rules towards national courts. Such a decentralization of the enforcement to national courts has proven to be necessary if EEC competition policy is to be effectively complied with by the various market operators. Litigation between them should be considered more normal than complaining to the Commission when disputes arise.

The Commission itself, after such a decentralization has taken effect, could make better use of its limited manpower by preparing and enacting legislation, by giving guidance in the system and by fixing the principles and the tendencies of EEC competition policy, rather than having to deal with numerous cases of complaints which can easily be dealt with by national courts. The Commission could then remain the central policy making institution. Only the application and enforcement of its policy is to be decentralized to the national courts, not the policy making powers themselves.

This would not prevent the Commission from making its point of view known, even in some of the cases before national courts, since the Commission makes a systematic use of the possibility to intervene whenever an interpretative procedure is submitted by a national court to the European Court of Justice under Article 177 of the EEC Treaty. The Commission even referred in its Thirteenth Competition Report to the possibilities of increased co-operation with national courts.[42]

3. Conclusions

Apart from a small number of gaps the system of competition law covers now all sectors of the economy of the European Community and has addressed most problems in the field of antitrust. When considering co-operation enterprises shall have to take into account the limits and procedures set out by this system. The way in which it evolves is, however, certainly not making such co-operation impossible.

---

[39] 1980 Wirtschaftsrecht 329 (23 October 1979).
[40] *L'Hourre v. Sipefel,* Bulletin des Arrêts de la Cour de Cassation, Chambre Civile 1982, vol. 2, at 69.
[41] *Garden Cottage Foods v. Milk Marketing Board,* (1983) 2 All ER 770.
[42] *Commission Thirteenth Report on Competition Policy 218* (1984).

Co-operation will not be judged exclusively on its effects on competition. The application of competition policy inserts itself in a broader framework of economic thinking. Other policies such as industrial policy, influence the final evaluation of the Commission in view of the overall objectives of the EEC Treaty.

This evaluation is more than legal alone. It also contains an economic assessment of the behaviour involved. Individual decisions of the Commission may contain a detailed analysis of the economic circumstances and background. On the legislative side the Commission enacts group exemption regulations, which can be tailored to the specific requirements of the industry concerned. Such group exemptions provide absolute legal protection. Agreements that fall within the scope of these group exemptions cannot be declared void. National courts can enforce competition rules and in particular give effect to these group exemptions. As the number of these group exemptions is steadily growing, more and more clarity is created in competition policy.

The enacting of legislation and the fixing of principles in important decisions in general, ensures that the Commission elaborates and applies a real competition policy which can be effectively enforced in a decentralized way through natural courts.

II. European competition rules – effective implementation

M. VAN EMPEL

1. Introduction

Why not start with a truism? No rule of law can hope to be respected which is not effectively implemented. Behind this truism, however, a more complex problem appears to be hidden. Effective implementation of the law depends on a more or less tacit understanding and cooperation between the authorities and the citizens. Purely in terms of efficiency, implementation should rely to a great extent on acceptance of the rule by the citizen to which it applies. Indeed, not only dictatorships have discovered that disregard of any such acceptance makes implementation into an uphill fight. On the other hand, acceptance by the citizen is in its turn always, at least to some extent, dependent upon a shared feeling that the rule is taken seriously by the authorities also. Thus, the authorities should be seen to stand by the rules they have enacted: they should be seen to respect those rules as binding upon themselves as well as to be prepared to take on anybody else infringing those rules. To be sure, the latter means that, if need be, massive reaction may be expected to follow massive infringement.

Whereas this seems to be true in essence for any rule of law, it would appear to be especially so with regard to rules governing economic competition in a decentralized economy, where enterprises are essentially left to their own wits. There, still more perhaps than elsewhere, relying exclusively on implementation by authority is simply without any perspective whatsoever. At the same time, precisely because the rules concerned are meant to affect the respective competitive positions of the enterprises concerned, these will only accept them as parameters for their own behaviour if they feel secure that they will be backed by the authorities, if need be, against any cheating on those rules by their competitors.

It is against this background that it is proposed to examine somewhat further how matters stand today with regard to the effective implementation of the rules on competition within the European Communities. In doing so, an attempt will be made to abstract somewhat from the purely legal approach, and to take due account of the perspective of the businessman who is, after all, the one whose acceptance of the rules is crucial to their effectiveness. By itself this perspective directly determines the terms of the discussion already. As a matter of fact, this means that the distinction

15

between the general regime of free competition and the special rules pertaining to certain specific sectors, which distinction comes naturally to lawyers familiar with Community law, should be seen as an issue rather than a fact. Indeed, in terms of acceptance of the rules as law, there is no obvious justification for such distinction and even the relatively well informed businessman may be excused for hoping – or even expecting-that what apparently is allowed in, say, agriculture or the steel-sector should be allowed in his particular line of business, also. Consequently, it is proposed to start the discussion here at what to lawyers might well seem to be the reverse end, i.e. those sectors and activities where 'special' rules apply, which are not based essentially on the concept of free competition between independent enterprises.

2. *Special sectors*

A. Agriculture

It is by now a well established tradition that for the agricultural sector not much faith is put on the working of the free market as a mechanism of economic coordination. In this, the EEC-policy is in substance no more than a continuation, on an enlarged geographical scale, of notions and concepts accepted by most, if not all Member States. As a matter of fact, disagreement over the Common Agricultural Policy in its present form, whatever its eventual outcome, is not likely to result in any overall 'abandonment' of farmers to the free forces of the market.

In official legal terms the reservations of the EEC with regard to the free competition-model find their expression in Article 42 of the Treaty, as implemented in Regulation 26/62. The provisions of that regulation leave quite some scope for discussion and some authoritive interpretation by the Court would therefore certainly be very welcome. Be that as it may, however, the overall picture presented by the Community policy on agriculture is clearly that of economic coordination through organization rather than through competition. In other words, it seems a fair statement that in this sector the tone is set by a sense of solidarity inside the sector, supported and even to a large extent guaranteed by public authority. Under those circumstances the enterprises concerned are apt to view full fledged competition as, at best, irrelevant and, at worst, a dangerous return to the bad old days.

It would seem that this view is more or less generally accepted. As a matter of fact, where the possible applicability of free competition-concepts is argued here at all, the discussion mostly boils down to the question as to what extent such application makes sense in situations which, exceptionally, are not determined by authority. This is mainly a matter of establishing the extent to which protection of the farmers (the core of the issue) requires extending the organization, either down-stream product-wise, or geographically. Those affected by such discussions may be forgiven for feeling that it is not really fair and reasonable where it is proposed to draw the line so as

16

to submit them to the regime of free competition whereas their parameters are in fact determined by agricultural organization by authority.

B. Transport

Of course, one should be wary of sweeping statements on the general state of mind of entire sectors of the economy. Nevertheless, it would seem that the attitude on the present issue – viz. that of coordination through organization versus competition – is in the transport-sector less averse of competition than is the case in agriculture. This is not contradicted by the well-known fact that in many subsectors of the transport-sector organizations which are guaranteed, sponsored or even simply owned by the State are rife. Indeed, whereas it seems safe to state that in agriculture organization of markets is essentially a bottom-upwards exercise on the initiative of the farmers, in transport the top-down public interest-input in the policy would appear to be relatively more pronounced. In general terms the picture is therefore that of a sector where hard-nosed individualistic competition is certainly a factor to be reckoned with, but where at the same time the scope for competitive action is limited, one way or the other.

How does this affect the attitude towards legal rules on free competition? In this regard, there would appear to be not much more hope for general acceptance – in the sense which we are concerned with here – of those rules than there is in agriculture. Certainly, it may be true that, of and by themselves, enterprises in the transport-sector are much more competition-minded than their colleagues in agriculture. They know very well however that, due to State intervention and supervision, their choice of weapons for the competitive struggle is severely limited. To put it bluntly, it frequently is more rewarding in competition-terms to have the ear of the transport-ministry than to cut prices (supposing the latter is allowed at all). Under those circumstances it is not very realistic to expect the enterprises concerned to put their faith – and money – with implementation of rules which are based on a concept of free market competition not shared by public authority.

The laborious developments of EEC law in this regard bear witness of this underlying attitude. The differences in jurisdiction from one transport-sector to another as laid down in the Treaty should not mask the fact that by and large public authorities are very reluctant to whole-heartedly accept the competition-concept for transport as such. For that reason alone and quite apart still from their own initial preferences, enterprises in that sector may not be expected to support implementation of an EEC competition law the actual impact of which in practice is very uncertain indeed.

C. Steel

A third major sector which is subject to a specific competition-regime is of course the steel-sector. Here the general attitude appears to be again different from that in the two sectors discussed earlier. For and by itself there seems to be no reason why steel should be any less competition-minded than other basic industries relying heavily on economies of scale. So it would appear that the factor which sets steel apart in this regard is history. It was long seen as the core of industrialization and therefore of such vital strategic importance to the nation as such that it should not be left at the mercy of competitive forces on the free market. It is well known that this same philosophy still was at the basis of the ECSC Treaty: as the German steel-industry was to be resuscitated on an 'organized' basis anyway, better have it organized under a supranational 'High Authority', together with the steel-industry of the other Member States. As a result European steel-industry took on certain traits of a regulated industry. Indeed, individual enterprises were told to compete amongst themselves (Art. 65 ECSC), but knew at the same time that the structural parameters of their market-behaviour were set by authority (merger control, crisis, penury).

Against this background it should not come as a surprise that when indeed the steel-industry was faced with a serious crisis of over-capacity, the solution was sought in an overall 'organization' of the industry with a view to an 'orderly' cut-back on capacity sponsored, and guaranteed by, the authority of the European Commission.

To be sure, whether as such this policy was good or bad should remain, in the present context, a moot question. The points at issue here are else-where. On the one hand, one cannot expect an industry which, for as long as anybody can remember, has operated within certain 'regulated' metes and bounds, to accept, let alone enthousiastically support, a free market concept and the legal competition-rules based thereon. Secondly, whereas steel certainly was, and to a large extent still is, a basic industry, there are other sectors who may claim with some justification to be in a similar position intrinsically. To this it is hardly a conclusive answer to point out that back in 1951 the six original Member States agreed that steel (and coal) should be a special case.

3. State regulation and state aids

The fact that the three major sectors mentioned above have consciously been awarded special treatment, and thus been isolated from application of competition-law generally, is already important enough, both in intrinsic terms and as a precedent for other, adjacent or (allegedly) similar, sectors of the economy. Nevertheless it could be argued in this regard that this does not affect the position of those sectors as an exception to the rule. It is therefore of perhaps still greater importance that also outside those specific sectors parameters for enterprise-action are perceived as not being deter-mined exclusively by competition, but also, to a more or less considerable extent, by conscious policy of public authorities. It is certainly true that

18

much State Regulation, which still fairly recently could be thought to raise formidable barriers to entry of 'undesirable' competitors, has been done away with (at the hands of the courts, rather than of the European Commission). Provisionally the result thereof is gradual liberalization of market entry. It remains to be seen however, to what extent such regulation as has been done away with on a national level, may perhaps be resuscitated on an EEC-wide level. To be sure, EEC-regulation of entry for the whole of the Common Market may be fine for the 'integration'-side of EEC-policy, but its effect on the model of free competition should also be kept in mind.

Whereas the 'negative' side of State regulation has thus been – at least for the time being – retracting under the influence of the EEC, the 'positive' side of it – State aids – have not only proved more untractable, but have even become more refined and varied over the last few years. The relatively straightforward loss-compensation for 'sunset-industries', which was rife in the 1970s, may have been hard to combat for the European Commission in social and political terms, its classification under the EEC Treaty did not raise much difficulty. Now that governments have switched to 'agressive' subsidizing of 'high tech' (in its various connotations), it has become much more difficult to draw the line. In the first place, is any specific contribution to enterprise-income by the State a subsidy which affects the latter's competitive position, or is it possible to distinguish 'pre-competitive' or 'para-competitive' contributions which escape scrutiny 'per se'? In the second place, in sofar as the EEC itself grants subsidies to certain individual enterprises – e.g. within the framework of ESPRIT and similar programmes – the European Commission may find it difficult to object to national subsidies on a related or similar basis. Thus, far from disappearing gradually from the scene as something of the past, overtaken by the Common Market, State subsidies may well appear, in the perception of the businessman, a continuously relevant element of his competitive position.

As a result it seems much more likely that enterprises will compete for the granting of subsidies, rather than fight them as contrary to the philosophy of the free market. In other terms, here again the conclusion must be that one should not be too optimistic as to the general acceptance by the enterprises concerned of what the lawyer sees as the basic rules of conduct for those enterprises.

4. International trade and dumping

There is a limit to the possible inconsistency which one can allow oneself in acclaiming free trade and competition internally, whilst raising barriers against imports from abroad. This is not in the first place a 'technical' proposition. Indeed, one might well imagine a system where, precisely because the internal market is shielded from the competition from abroad, the authorities insist on a vigorous internal competition. As a matter of fact, this is but the reverse of the classic statement that small 'open' economies do not need a competition-policy as any entrenched positions will be quickly swept away by imports anyway.

It is submitted, however, that the real problem lies elsewhere. Again, the point at issue is the attitude and the perception of the businessman. Obviously, what matters to the individual enterprise is competition as such. It is of only secondary importance to it whether that competition is home-made or originates abroad. Thus, where home-based enterprises lobby for restriction of imports, they presumably do so, not because they like 'internal' competition any more than competition from abroad, but in order to restrict competition as such. In a sense the single major aspect which distinguishes foreign competition from internal competition is the fact that on average it is more difficult to come to terms with a foreign competitor than with a fellow-countryman. And the impact of foreign competition goes beyond the direct confrontation of one offer with another. A major well-known effect of an 'outsider' on a market is the additional uncertainty he creates amongst the various 'insiders', who do not know how each of them will react to this external pressure. Therefore, eliminating such external pressure takes care not only of the 'direct' problem (the pressure each 'insider' feels himself), but also of the 'indirect' problem, viz. the uncertainty which stands in the way of a proper understanding between the home-based enterprises.

This should be kept in mind when considering EEC-policy with regard to international trade. That the Common Agricultural Policy with its emphasis on organization has as a necessary complement the isolation from the world market through variable levies has been sufficiently stressed time and again. It should be noted, however, that in other economic sectors similar results are brought about where the EEC market is shielded from the impact of foreign competition. This is especially true for anti-dumping levies, which, after all, in essence operate similarly to the agricultural levies in that they also are meant to bridge the difference between the price offered by the 'outsider' and the pricelevel deemed acceptable by the 'insiders' in the EEC. It would be probably be going too far to say that the mere joint filing of a dumping-complaint by a European industry-organization would imply already of necessity the kind of agreement which Article 85 EEC would in principle prohibit. It is, however, submitted here that serious consideration should be given to the fact that a successful anti-dumping action eliminates not only the alleged dumping as such, but also the uncertainty which for the various 'insiders' exists about their respective reactions to the pressure on the market brought to bear by the 'dumping' outsider. Against this background one should be not too surprised that European industry interprets the recent wave of 'Japan-bashing' as a signal that also for purely 'internal' relations on the Common Market the authorities in Brussels will not insist on the 'uncoordinated' uncertainty implied in the free market competition model.

This is the more so as at the same time this policy on international trade is

20

complemented by a Research & Development-policy (ESPRIT and the like) which declared purpose it is to promote the competitive position of European industry *vis-à-vis* their rivals overseas. A coordinated effort to launch European 'champions' in the international contest for world-markets leaves relatively little room for a vigorous competition-policy at home.

5. *Provisional conclusions*

At this stage it seems possible to draw a few provisional conclusions.

In the first place there is reasonable doubt as to whether the view fairly generally held by lawyers, to the effect that free competition is the rule and 'organization' no more than the exception, is indeed the valid one when it comes to acceptance in the field. Obviously – to play with words for a while – businessmen want to be free from free competition if it suits them in competition. But lawyers should be wary of dismissing this as no more than a crude free-booter's philosophy. Indeed, the few examples mentioned above may be taken as an indication that in many instances those businessmen may well find support in declared government-policies. To this it is no answer that public authorities happen to be organized in various departments whose respective responsibilities will lead, one to stress the competition-model, another to prefer a more organized approach. Where public authority arrogates to it the right and the duty to set limits to the freedom of action of individual economic actors, those actors should not be expected to integrate those limits in *their* own policy-making, unless public authority proves itself capable of integrating them in *its* own policy-making, itself. Where public authority does not live up to that expectation, the rule-exception relationship between free competition and organization is, at least, less absolute than generally assumed by lawyers, and possibly even reversed altogether.

This possible reversal of truths is in itself already worrysome enough. There is, however, still another complication. As a matter of fact, the level of 'juridification' of the rules appears to be, on average, clearly different for free competition as compared with organization by authority. Whereas the former lends itself relatively easily to more or less abstract, generally formulated, rules, the latter is, almost by definition, the result of a case-by-case approach, where discretionary power of the administration is relatively wide, in practice if not necessarily in principle. This means that in effect this is not merely a matter of preferring one approach over the other, but also of putting into jeopardy – at least to some extent – the rule of law. As it is, all this appears to apply in the EEC just as it does elsewhere. Of course, even in the regulated sectors such as agriculture, transport and steel, even with state aids and protectionism in international trade, the authorities will strive to insert their policy-decisions in a consistent body of legal rules. In practice, however the variations over the years appear to take over.

Within the specific framework of the EEC the problems (for the lawyers)

21

are still further enhanced by the fact that much of this discretionary power is wielded by national authorities of the Member States. In most cases mentioned above this needs no further elaboration. Even for agriculture, however, it can be argued that the CAP on the one hand is based upon a steadily renegotiated compromise between national discretionary policies, and on the other hand in practical implementation leaves considerable room for the latter also.

Thus, taking all in all, where they are looking for general acceptance of the rules, lawyers should do well to take into account the possibility that the instances of 'organization by authority', rather than being 'islands in a sea of antitrust' are in fact seen by those directly concerned in practice as a forest (where one has to learn to find one's way, but where cover is always available) with a few open spaces in between, where suddenly one risks finding oneself uncovered to free competition.

6. Competition law proper

Having thus established that probably free competition is less absolute and general a principle of the Common Market than a strictly legal approach would have it, let us now see how serious EEC Competition Law takes itself. In other words, how comprehensive and consistent are the free competition rules where they do apply? Again, the answer to that question lies first of all with the public authorities concerned. It is only to the extent that these are prepared to put their authority behind effective implementation of, and respect for, the rules that they can expect businessmen to take the latter seriously.

Some eight years ago, at a similar occasion at Leyden University, I was given the opportunity to discuss this same question.[1] I then found that there was considerable risk in setting too great store on application of Article 85, paragraph 3, EEC as an effective instrument of competition. Rather, more emphasis should be laid on the role of national courts, which meant i.a. that one should also be prepared to leave more room for a 'rule of reason' with regard to Article 85, paragraph 1, EEC.[2]

I cannot help feeling that developments since then have borne me out, at

---

[1] *See* M van Empel, 'Rechter en administratie in het Europese mededingingsbeleid', SEW 1980, p. 32.

[2] *See* on the 'rule of reason' in EEC competition law: R. Joliet, 'The Rule of Reason in Anti-trust Law', 1967; B. Hawk, 'EEC and U.S. Competition Policies-Contrast and Convergence, in *Enterprise Law of the 80's,* 1980, 48; M.C. Schechter, 'The Rule of Reason in European Competition Law', L.I.E.I., 1982, 1; I. Forrester and Ch. Norall, 'The Laicization of Community Law: Self-help and the Rule of Reason: How competition-law is and could be applied', C.M.L. Rev., 1984, 13. V. Korah, 'The Rise and Fall of Provisional Validity – The Need for a Rule of Reason in EEC Anti-trust', *Northwestern Journal of International Law & Business,* 1981, 340; R. Kovar, 'Le droit communautaire de la concurrence et la "règle de raison"', RTDE 1987, 237.

least to some extent. Obviously, there is still much opposition to the notion of a 'rule of reason'. It is therefore frequently argued that those cases which could be interpreted as instances of such a 'rule of reason' are either exceptions to the rule or can be explained in terms of mere 'economic' reading of Article 85. However, it would seem that we are thus getting dangerously close to pure semantics. When suggesting a 'rule of reason', it is by no means necessarily implied that by that same token the American 'rule of reason' as it has been developed there by the courts, should be transplanted to Europe, lock, stock and barrel. A 'rule of reason' here should be a European 'rule of reason' which fits in the specific EEC framework, and more particularly takes due account of the fact that after all there is the provision of Article 85, paragraph 3, and the exclusive powers of the European Commission in that regard. But then the reverse is also true: where in too many cases decisions on the basis of the exclusive power of Article 85, paragraph 3, are simply not taken, be they positive or negative, the situation has to be sorted out, one way or the other. It is against this background that a 'rule of reason' offers itself as a possible solution. To put it bluntly: where the Commission deals with a mere few dozen cases a year, practical needs will dictate other solutions than those envisaged originally. Or, as it was put recently by Judge *Koopmans*, the 'orthodox view will be more difficult to maintain the more pronounced is the Commission's passivity *vis-à-vis* new developments'.[3]

Of course the major problem which the possible admission of a 'rule of reason' presents to the Commission is that it might thereby lose overall control over implementation of Article 85 EEC altogether. Indeed, where the courts find that Article 85, paragraph 1, does not apply, discussion as to a possible exemption by the Commission simply does not arise, in the first place. For that reason the Commission, which of course is also fully aware of the dilemma mentioned by Judge *Koopmans*, has sought other solutions which, whilst taking care of the 'mass-problem', would still leave it in control of implementation of the rules on competition. This would seem to be the origin for, on the one hand its drive for a 'decentralized' competition-policy and, on the other hand its enhanced enthusiasm for 'block-exemption regulations'. The question therefore now is: how adequate are those solutions?

7. Decentralization

Decentralization as a declared policy of the Commission first came out in the open in its Thirteenth Report,[4] in which it explicitly called for an

---

[3] See T. Koopmans, 'De plaats van het kartelrecht in het EEG-Verdrag, SEW 1987, p. 424 (at 427) (my translation, vE).
[4] Commission of the European Communities, *Thirteenth Report on Competition Policy* (1984), Introduction at p. 13.

enhanced role of national courts in the implementation of EEC competition law. As a policy statement this certainly is of some importance. The Commission openly recognizes that it is not in a position to claim an exclusive position as the guardian of the competition rules, as it more or less openly appeared to do in the past. True, it may be supposed that national courts have in the meantime become more knowledgeable in the intricacies of EEC law and therefore can now be better 'trusted' to take the right decisions in this field. Moreover, the Commission is presently working on a 'guide' for the courts to coach them still further. Nevertheless, with due respect it would seem that it is rather a change in Brussels than in the national courts which has spurred this development. The Commission has apparently come to accept that under the current staffing-conditions it simply has to tone down its role in day-to-day implementation.

Still, the exact implications of this shift in emphasis for the practical implementation of the competition-rules are as yet unclear. As far as Article 85 is concerned, the Commission's exclusive jurisdiction under paragraph 3 remains unaffected. This means that, unless and in sofar as block exemptions are issued (*see infra*), decentralization if any should make itself felt in the application of paragraph 1. Now, as mentioned above there is no sign that 'decentralization' implies a shift in the views held by the Commission on a possible 'rule of reason'. When going by statements made by representatives of the Commission's services, one gathers that the Commission sees 'decentralization' essentially as an exercise in which it itself takes all the major policy-decisions whereas the national courts are confined to mere application and implementation of well established rules in run-of-the-mill cases. One suspects that the same holds true, if not more, where application of Article 86 would be concerned.

The question is, however, whether this is going to work. To be effective, statements of policy have to be implemented in practice. And practice here is essentially triggered, not by autonomous action by the authorities, be they EEC or national, but rather by the enterprises concerned. These, up till now have been accustomed to go mostly to the Commission when they felt aggrieved by a restraint of competition. True, in the past they could feel actually welcomed by the Commission, but the main advantage was that a complaint in Brussels was much less costly and in many instances more quickly effective than national court-proceedings. This means that for 'decentralization' to work, something would have to change in that underlying cost-benefit ratio. In other words, the route via the Commission should be made less attractive and/or the route via the national courts should be made more attractive. The problem for the Commission now is that ideally, for implementation of EEC law to be effective, it should only send away plaintiffs when it can be sure that their case will be picked up effectively by the national court concerned. Otherwise, the credibility of the system might drop quickly and dramatically. In this light one should not be surprised if the Commission makes its 'negative' action in this regard tributary to progress on the 'positive' front in the national courts. At this side also, however, the situation is a complex one. In the first place, of course, the situation differs substantially from one country to another (and the Commission cannot be seen to trust the courts of one Member State more than those of another). But even – or precisely – the courts which are knowledgeable in EEC competition law might have difficulty in fulfilling the expectations which the Commission has in their regard. As a matter of fact, in actual court-practice the distinction made by the Commission between well-established rules and new developments is probably not very effective. It is the lawyers' stock in trade to argue, one, that the known rule should apply, the other, that it should be distinguished. The courts and the Commission may well agree on the more extreme examples, one way or the other. The whole concept could not get off the ground really, however, if the national courts would not have substantial room for their own independent judgement as to which cases should be deemed 'new' and therefore should be referred to the Commission. As such, a basis for such approach has been laid already in the Haecht II-judgment of the Court of Justice.[5] The difference would be one of emphasis: the courts should not only decide the case where they feel that they know what the Commission would have decided in their place, but also where the decision depends on their own judgement of the merits under Articles 85 and 86. Without such shift in emphasis 'decentralization' would remain an empty slogan. With it, however, it is hard to see what would be the difference with a 'rule of reason' in the sense as indicated above.

It is therefore submitted that 'decentralization' offers no real way out of the dilemma which the Commission faces. Indeed, either it does not solve the problem because the courts would be too timid, or it replaces one problem by another, because the courts would take over much of the actual implementation which the Commission would have liked to keep for itself. Under the circumstances it seems a fair guess that the Commission will consider the former the lesser evil (here again doubts on the consistency of the courts' approach in the various Member States may well play their role). If that guess proves correct we should not set great store on the contribution that a deliberate policy of 'decentralization' as such (apart from the specific regime of the block exemptions) can make to an improvement of the implementation of the rules on competition in the EEC. The Commission would then probably continue to call for a more active role of the national courts whilst at the same time effectively blocking any such development, by not sending away plaintiffs in any substantial numbers.

8. Block-exemptions

When discussing 'decentralization' above, a reservation has been made for the specific regime of the block exemptions. Indeed, it can be said that,

[5] Case 48/73, *Brasserie de Haecht v. Wilkin-Janssen,* 6 March 1973, ECR 1973, page 77.

whatever the merits of 'decentralization' as a more general policy, block exemptions provide a clear illustration of a division of jurisdiction between the Commission and the national courts. As a matter of fact, there can be no doubt that by enacting a block-exemption the Commission has 'exhausted' its exclusive right under Article 85, paragraph 3. Precisely because the Commission has chosen to formulate generally applicable rules, the actual application of those rules to the case at hand is left to the parties concerned and, where necessary, to the courts. Therefore, both the parties concerned and the courts themselves will see it as the responsibility of the courts to settle any questions which the interpretation and application of the block-exemptions might raise (possibly with the guidance of the Court of Justice under Article 177 EEC). By that same token the Commission's role in the field covered by a block-exemption becomes a marginal one. It is in fact confined to, on the one hand, the 'opposition procedure' in the more recent block-exemptions (which actually is about agreements not covered by the explicit provisions of the regulation concerned) and, on the other hand, the 'abuse procedure' on the basis of which the Commission can withdraw the exemption by an individual decision (no instance of its actual use is known to me).

Ideally, this arrangement meets the Commission's preoccupations. Indeed, it allows for the Commission to take all the major policy-decisions whilst leaving the burden of day-to-day implementation to the parties concerned and, where need be, to the national courts. As it is, the early block exemptions appear to have complied with this pattern. More recently, however, the situation in this regard is much less clear. The difference stems from the fact that, whereas the earlier block exemptions were essentially a consolidating exercise, the more recent ones apparently are meant to break new ground in policy terms. Illustrative of this point is a comparison of Regulation 67/67 with the block-exemption for franchise agreements as currently envisaged. Regulation 19/65 provided the legal basis for both, and thus for both the requirement, as laid down in the recitals of that regulation, that the Commission should acquire first practical experience with individual cases before drafting a block-exemption, equally applied. With due respect, it would seem that this requirement is taken very lightly by the Commission in the more recent exercise over franchise agreements. For the issue under discussion here this difference of approach has important implications. Regulation 67/67 concerned a fairly strictly defined and homogeneous category of contracts and was based upon practical experience by the Commission, as required by Regulation 19/65. Under such conditions the repartition of jurisdiction between the Commission and the national courts comes fairly close to the 'ideal' arrangement as indicated above: the Commission takes the general policy-decisions, whereas the courts look after the daily implementation. On the contrary, the more recent regulations are generally concerned with much more complex relationships, such as e.g. R & D cooperation, franchising and know how. In good logic this might be ex-

26

pected to induce the Commission to acquire still more practical experience in individual cases before embarking on the drafting of a block exemption. On the contrary, the general impression of the Commission's attitude on this point rather is one of impatience with the 'hard slogging' of individual decisions and the clear wish to take general policy decisions quickly. (To be fair, the Commission is encouraged in this approach by insistent calls for 'legal security' addressed to it by a number of organizations of trade and industry.) Now, whatever the merits of this approach under the 'enabling' regulations on which these block exemptions are based in law, the inevitable consequence of it is that the 'modern' block exemptions are relatively vague and leave therefore much room for interpretation, and thus in effect for policy-decisions. And, as indicated above, under the arrangement of the block exemptions responsibility for those decisions lies primarily with the national courts.

It would appear, therefore, that the more recent regulations which the Commission has enacted in this field with a view to clearly spelling out a policy, imply in fact an abandonment by the Commission of a substantial part of its implementation-powers to the benefit of the national courts. When enterprises concerned will be looking for guidance on their position under those regulations the national courts, rather than the Commission will in fact be responsible for the answer.

It is submitted here that it is essential that this development be recognized as such. The Commission certainly has an arguable case for its current policy on block exemptions. Why not accept then that there is also a price to be paid in terms of accepting an enhanced and more independent role for the national courts? That role may of course give rise to certain problems. But – again a truism – problems are not solved by pretending that they do not exist. It is obvious to all concerned that some sort of co-operation is required between the Commission and the national courts in this field. But for such co-operation to be a lasting and constructive one it should be based on the equality of the parties concerned.

9. The new 'Court of First Instance'

At this place it seems appropriate to say a few words on the new 'Court of First Instance' as envisaged in the revision of the EEC Treaty (the 'Single Act').[6] As a matter of fact, that court would i.a. be responsible for hearing cases brought against the Commission in competition-matters. At the moment of writing it is still far from certain when and under what conditions this new judiciary body will start its activities. It would seem likely, how-

---

[6] *See* articles 4, 11 and 26 of the 'European Single Act (Luxembourg, 17 February 1986, The Hague, 28 February 1986).

27

ever, that if anything it will reinforce the trends mentioned above. Indeed, the declared purpose of the creation of the new 'instance' is to provide a forum in which the decisions of the Commission can be fully scrutinized on substance. The obvious consequence would therefore be a substantial increase in the workload of the Commission services. In the first place, the mere fact of having to defend in detail its findings of fact before a critical forum will take up a lot of time in itself. Moreover, whatever the present level of drafting and reasoning in the Commission-decisions, it may be safely assumed that the 'new court' will concentrate the Commission's mind still more than before. Thus, other things being equal, the burden of taking individual decisions will thereby increase, and the enthusiasm at the Commission for such individual decisions will decrease further accordingly. In other words the relative importance of the approach by regulation may be expected to increase still further.

10. Conclusions

Where does this leave us with regard to implementation of EEC competition-law proper? The overall picture would appear to be that of the Commission slowly and gradually retreating into a position of a 'legislative' authority, leaving most of the ground of actual day-to-day implementation to the national courts. At present this is not likely to be a popular thesis. Indeed, it is a well-known fact that the Commission cherishes its executive role under competition-law as one of the few areas where it is really on its own *vis-à-vis* EEC-citizens. Moreover, probably most EEC lawyers will support the Commission on this. It is submitted, however, that legal principles and severe fines in a few individual cases cannot mask the fact that on a market of some 300 million people an executive which confines itself to a few dozen individual decisions a year cannot seriously claim to be the only instance which takes policy-decisions on the implementation of the competition rules. As a matter of fact, the gist of what has been said above is that, in practice, if not in theory, the Commission has come round to accepting this as a fact of life. The problem is that as long as what is now ever more becoming the rule is still treated as if it were the exception, it will be difficult to realize an efficient and effective implementation of competition law. It will be only when the role of the national courts is fully recognized, not only as one of taking care of the crumbs off the table of the Commission, but rather as a full-blown partner with its own responsibilities and which therefore is entitled to its own free judgement, that one can hope for a balanced and consistent system of implementation. And this in its turn is a condition for the general acceptance of competition law by those directly concerned, i.e. the enterprises on the Common Market.

For the present, conclusions as to the effective implementation of competition law within the EEC are hardly positive, all in all. It has been found that the sway which free competition holds over the economy on the Common Market is less general than is suggested by the rule-exception relationship laid down in the Treaties. Moreover, where the rules of free competition do apply, the system of implementation would seem to be getting into disarray. Where the official distribution of power and jurisdiction is perceived as being almost counterproductive in terms of actual individual decisions taken, the acceptance of the rules by those directly concerned with actual practice 'in the field' is at risk.

III.   Shipping and competition

P.J. SLOT

1.   Introduction

On 22 December 1986 the Council of Ministers of the European Economic Community adopted four regulations[1] concerning maritime transport. Together the four regulations constitute an important step towards a common maritime transport policy. The package had been prepared in a Commission communication of 14 March 1985 entitled 'Progress towards the common transport policy – maritime transport'.[2] From a point of view of a common maritime transport policy the four regulations should be studied and analyzed together. From the point of view of a competition lawyer however, the competition regulation is an interesting example of a sectoral application of Articles 85 and 86 of the Treaty. This regulation presents many peculiar features for which one will look in vain in other regulations which give effect to the principles of Articles 85 and 86. These reasons amply justify a separate discussion of regulation 4056/86.

Shortly after the enactment of Regulation no. 17 the Council issued Regulation no. 141.[3] The latter regulation exempted transport from the application of Regulation no. 17.[4] The preamble of Regulation no. 141 noted that for the inland transport sector the application of Articles 85 and 86 was to be expected shortly. For sea and air transport it could not be foreseen whether and when such application would be enacted. The optimism regarding the prompt application to inland transport has not been wholly justified. Regulation 1017/67[5] applying Articles 85 and 86 to the inland transport sector

---

[1] Council Regulations 4055/86, applying the freedom to provide services to maritime transport between Member States and between Member States and third countries; 4056/86 laying down detailed rules for the application of Articles 85 and 86 of the Treaty to maritime transport; 4057/86 on unfair pricing practices in maritime transport; 4058/86 concerning coordinated action to safeguard free access to cargoes in ocean trades; OJ 1986 L 378.
[2] Document COM (85) 90 final.
[3] Council Regulation no. 141 of 26 November 1962 exempting transport from the application of Council Regulation no. 17 (OJ 1962, no. 124, page 2751.)
[4] Council Regulation no. 17 of 6 February 1962, First Regulation implementing Articles 85 and 86 of the Treaty (OJ 1962, no. 13, page 204).
[5] Council Regulation 1017/68 of 19 July 1968 applying rules of competition to transport by rail, road, and inland waterway (OJ 1968 L 175, page 1.)

was enacted in 1967. Regulation no. 141 exempted shipping and air transport from the application of Regulation no. 17 for an indefinite period.

Twenty four years passed before the present regulation was enacted. It is striking that sea and air transport have been able to withstand the application of Articles 85 and 86 so long. There are several reasons for this.

1. For a long time it was debated whether the general rules of the Treaty and in particular Articles 85 and 86 apply to shipping. The judgment of the Court in the Asjes Case[6] finally decided this matter.
2. A particular characteristic of sea and air transport has always been the importance of the international dimension. This makes the drafting of a regulation for competition rules very difficult. Furthermore, the example set by the Shipping Act of the United States and its application by the Federal Maritime Commission and the Courts have made shipowners very wary of competition rules.[7] This example has led West-European shipowners to fight competition rules for a very long time.
3. The informal character of the industry has forestalled the application of Articles 85 and 86. In the shipping industry the interests of shipowners and shippers are often closely connected. Loyalty rebates are very common in times of recession. There is ample consultation between shipowners and shippers and it is highly institutionalised. There is a 'official code of practices'[8] jointly drafted by the Council of European Shipowners Association (Cemza) and the European Shippers Council (ESC). These closely knit relations explain why shippers seldom go to court to solve disputes with shipowners. The court action that finally shed light on the relation of Articles 85 and 86 to shipping, was not a shipping case but an air transport case. Ironically the judgment of the Court in the Asjes Case came when agreement on a regulation applying Articles 85 and 86 to shipping was nearing. The Asjes Case is not only important for air transport, which does not yet have its competition regulation, but also for shipping. This is because some modes of maritime transport are excluded from the application of the regulation.

The developments that have finally caused the acceptance of the present regulation can be summarized as follows:

---

[6] Joint Cases 209-213/84, *Ministère Publique v. Asjes* ('Nouvelles Frontières'), 30 April 1986, ECR 1986, page 1425.

[7] *See* for instance: Faucett, F., and D.C. Nolan. US ocean shipping: the history, development and decline of the Conference Antitrust Exemption, *Northwestern Journal of International Law and Business* 1979, page 537 and:
Agman, R.S. Competition, rationalisation and US shipping policy. B, *Journal of Maritime Law and Commerce* (1976), page 1.

[8] Code of Practice for Conferences, joint publication of the Council of European and Japanese National Shipowners' Associations and the European National Shippers' Councils, adopted Genoa, October 1971, amended Copenhagen, April 1975.

1. The necessity to complement the Code of Conduct for liner conferences.[9]
2. The extent of the application of the Articles 85 and 86 to shipping and air transport had been clarified in the judgment of the Court in the Asjes Case.
3. The recent developments in the relations with the United States.
4. The Community has increasingly felt the need to develop instruments for an external policy.
5. The decline of the merchant marine of the countries of the European Community increased the necessity to develop a common transport policy.
6. The development of the competition policy in the inland transport sector reallayed the fears of an excessive application of competition policy.

Ad 1

After the enactment of Regulation 954/79[10] the Code had been accepted and incorporated in the legal order of the Community, but the fundamental gap between the Code and Articles 85 and 86 remained. The present competition regulation is first and foremost intended to grant conferences a block exemption. In that way the incompatibility between the Code and Articles 85 and 86 is taken away. As such the present regulation may be viewed as one of the recent block exemption regulations.

Ad 2

An increasing awareness that Articles 85 and 86 did apply to shipping makes individual court actions more likely. Until judgment in the Asjes Case it was not clear whether agreements would be automatically void according to Article 85, paragraph 2. It was clear however, that the Commission lacked the power to grant exemptions under Article 85, paragraph 3.

Ad 3

The shipping relations between the United States and the countries of Western Europe have been under strain since the 1950s. At the heart of the dispute, were fundamentally opposing views as to what sort of shipping policy should be adopted. The United States, guided by their anti-trust philosophy, had a very strong regulatory system especially concerning liner shipping. The countries of Western Europe adopted a traditionally 'laissez faire' policy. There had been regular talks between the United States and the countries of Western Europe to discuss this controversy. In the end, such discussions have never been very fruitful because the United States have always been very reluctant to come to certain agreements: for example

---

[9] United Nations Conference of Plenipotentiaries on a Code of Conduct for Liner Conferences (UN Publ., Sales no. E. 75. II), hereafter referred to as 'the Code'.

[10] Council Regulation 954/79 of 15 May 1979 Concerning the ratification by Member States at, or their accession to, the United Nations Convention on a Code of Conduct for Liner Conferences (OJ 1979 L 121, page 1).

concerning rebates or the discrimination of shippers. Furthermore, the United States have consistently pointed out that the countries in Western Europe would lack the necessary instruments to implement such agreements. To remedy such a situation would only be possible if Western European nations would develop their own instruments. Among such instruments was the application of Articles 85 and 86 to shipping.

Ad 4
Recently, international shipping relations have come under great strain. Several developing countries have severely restricted the competition in international shipping. These unilateral actions have largely been the result of a desire to protect national cargo shares due under the Code of Conduct or bilateral treaties. To the extent that the share of the conferences in the trade would decrease it would undermine the national cargo share. In this context it should be noted that owing to several developments in world shipping the position of conferences in many trades has come increasingly under pressure. Community shipowners, whether or not organized in conferences, and to some extent also Community shippers, have been complaining increasingly about the policy of certain developing countries. These complaints have finally led to an effort to develop an instrument to counter such policies at the level of the Community.

Ad 5
Apart from the developments described under 3 and 4, the sharp decline of the merchant marine of the European Community gave rise to a call for a Community maritime transport policy. In such a policy the application of Articles 85 and 86 could play an essential role to counter external pressure.

Ad 6
Contrary to sea and air transport the inland transport sector has seen the application of Articles 85 and 86 within a couple of years after the enactment of Regulation no. 17. After studying the effects of the application of the competition rules to the inland transport it became clear that competition policy need not be very harsh. Regulation no. 1017/68 apart from an exemtion for technical agreements, provided for a broad block exemption. Competition policy in the inland transport sector cannot be characterized as very burdensome. The first action of the Commission took place in 1985 with the enactment of the EATE decision.[11] Furthermore, actions before national courts have not been common after the enactment of the regulation. It should be noted, however, that such a notable absence of national

---

[11] Commission Decision 85/383/EEC of 10 July 1985 (IV/31.029-French inland waterway charter traffic: EATE levy) OJ 1985 L 219, page 35; Decision upheld in Case 272/85 *Association Nationale des Travailleurs Indépendants de la Batellerie (ANTIB) v. Commission*, 20 May 1987, not yet reported.

court actions may have been influenced by the exemption for technical agreements and the ample block exemption. On the whole, discussions in national administrations between officials responsible for sea transport have been influenced by the experiences of their colleagues in the inland transport sector. Furthermore, it should be noted that transport is increasingly multimodal. The effect of this is that from the shippers' point of view there is very little reason to apply competition rules to one mode and not to another mode of transport. A final point that is worth noting is that the exemption of Regulation no. 141 is limited to transport only. Ancillary and connected services are not covered by the exemption. This can be seen from the Commission's decision concerning Olympic Airways of 1985.[12] This point is important because it will not always be possible to delineate the relevant product markets. The Olympic Airways decision has created uncertainty in the sea and air transport industry. It made people wonder how far the immunity under Regulation no. 141 would actually extend.[13]

2. Main characteristics of the regulation

One of the most important issues in the discussion of the present regulation has always been its scope. A first question was whether the regulation should cover both in- and outbound traffic. The discussion was fuelled by the fear of being accused of extraterritorial legislation. It led several Member States to plead for a regulation limiting itself to outbound traffic. Rather less practical was the proposal to limit the scope of the regulation to c.i.f. agreements. The solution finally adopted is to apply the regulation to maritime transport services to or from Community ports. It should however immediately be noted that this extensive scope is accompanied by a safety valve to regulate conflicts of international law. Such a mechanism is contained in Article 9 and to some extent in Article 7, paragraph 2.

The next question was whether to limit the scope of the regulation to liner transport or to extend it to all maritime transport. It has been clear from the beginning that the regulation would cover liner transport *in toto* and that it would not be restricted to conferences only. Conference-only regulation is found in Canada, the United States and Australia. From the point of view of competition policy it would have been logical to extend the scope of the regulation to all maritime transport. After all, sea and air transport are the only sectors of the Community industry which are not covered by a regulation applying Articles 85 and 86. This logic has not been followed. In the beginning the Commission indicated that it needed more studies concerning

[12] Commission Decision 85/121/EEC of 23 January 1985 (IV/C/31.163-Olympic Airways) OJ 1985 L 46 page 51; Significantly, this decision was not challenged before the Court.
[13] Commission Decision of 13 July 1987 (IV/31.764 – Baltic International Freight Futures Exchange Limited) OJ 1987 L 222/24

the bulk sector. The preamble states that it appears preferable to exclude tramp vessel services from the scope of their regulation, rates for these services being freely negotiated on a case-by-case basis in accordance with supply and demand conditions. These arguments are not very convincing. The above enumerated arguments for the application of Articles 85 and 86 to shipping in general apply to the bulk sector as well. It has been argued that there are no cartels in the bulk sector. The fact is that even if this were true, it does not logically make sense. If there are no cartels why then should one object to the application of Articles 85 and 86. More importantly, it may be argued that the bulk sector does know some cartels. Especially long term contracts for the maritime transport of certain important primary commodities have features that may fall foul of Article 85, paragraph 1. Rumour has it that one of the Member States maintained strong opposition against including the bulk sector. The exclusion of the bulk sector from the scope of the regulation implies that in this sector the provisional validity of agreements as pronounced in the judgment in the Asjes Case will remain in force. Furthermore, the Commission lacks powers to apply Article 85, paragraph 3, in this sector. It would have been stronger to argue that the international character of the bulk sector warrants its exclusion. To a greater extent than in liner shipping bulk shipping is governed by the international market. Suffice to point to the very strong international character of the supply side. The majority of the bulk transport is carried out under flags of convenience. Furthermore, legislation in Canada, the United States and Australia also excludes the bulk sector.

Article 1, paragraph 3, of the regulation defines bulk transport as:

'tramp vessel services' means the transport of goods in bulk or in break-bulk in a vessel chartered wholly or partly to one or more shippers on the basis of a voyage or time charter or any other form of contract for non-regularly scheduled or non-advertised sailing where the freight rates are freely negotiated case by case in accordance with the conditions of supply and demand.

The original Commission proposal excluded bulk transport without further definition of the scope of the regulation. The present definition allows for a clear distinction between liner and bulk transport. In particular bulk transport in liner vessels is now covered by the regulation. The original proposal did not address this matter. Even though the regulation or its premable does not say so it should be assumed that tramp vessel services also include offshore services, deep sea towage and supply and salvage operations. In other words, such services are also excluded from the scope of the regulation.

Furthermore, the regulation only covers sea transport and not connected services such as stevedores and freight forwarders. This is contrary to Regulation 1017/67. It should also be noted that inland transport connecting with the sea leg is covered by Regulation 1017/67. The regulation does not fit

36

the usual pattern of Regulation no. 17 and Regulation 1017/67. Contrary to Article 1 of Regulation no. 17 and the Articles 2 and 7 of Regulation 1017/67 there is no explicit provision saying that agreements shall be prohibited as incompatible with the Common Market, no prior decision to that effect being required. Curiously enough, Article 8 of the present regulation does say that the abuse of a dominant position within the meaning of Article 86 shall be prohibited without a prior decision being required. Notwithstanding this omission it should be assumed that Article 85, paragraph 1, is directly applicable. The procedure laid down in Article 12 for application for an individual exemption under Article 85, paragraph 3 of the Treaty would not make sense otherwise. Nevertheless this omission does create uncertainty. This point will be further discussed below where Article 12 is reviewed.

Like Regulation 1017/68, there is an exemption for technical agreements. Article 85, paragraph 1, shall not apply to agreements etc. which have as sole object and effect to achieve technical improvements or co-operation by means of separately enumerated practices and agreements. This is laid down in Article 2 of the regulation.

Article 3 lays down the exemption for agreements between carriers concerning the operation of scheduled maritime transport services. The exemption practically condones the present conference practices. Agreements which have as their objective the fixing of rates and conditions of carriage and as the case may be, one or more of the following objectives:

A. the coordination of shipping timetables, sailing dates or dates of calls;
B. the determination of frequency of sailing or calls;
C. the coordination of allocation of sailing calls among members of the conference;
D. the regulation of the carrying capacity offered by each member;
E. the allocation of cargo or revenue among members.

There is only one condition attached to the exemption. Article 4 requires conferences to refrain from causing detriment to certain ports, transport users or carriers by applying for the carriage of the same good and in the area covered by the agreement, rates and conditions which differ according to country of origin or destination or to port of loading or discharge, unless such rates or conditions can be economically justified. Agreements not complying with the condition shall be automatically void.

Apart from this condition the exemption is subject to certain obligations.

1. There shall be consultations for the purpose of seeking solutions on issues of principle between transport users on the one hand and conferences on the other concerning the rates, conditions and quality of scheduled maritime transport services. These consultations shall take place whenever requested by any of the above mentioned parties.
2. Loyalty arrangements.

37

The shipping lines, members of a conference shall be entitled to institute and maintain loyalty arrangements with transport users, the form and terms of which shall be matters for consultation between the conference and transport users organizations. These loyalty arrangements shall provide safeguards making explicit the rights of transport users and conference members. These arrangements shall be based on the contract system or any other system which is also lawful.

Loyalty arrangements must offer transport users a system of immediate rebates or the choice between such a system and a system of deferred rebates. Furthermore the conference shall indicate which cargo is covered by the arrangements and a list of circumstances in which transport users are released from their loyalty obligation.

3. Services not covered by the freight charges.
Transport users shall be entitled to approach the undertakings of their choice in respect of inland transport operations and quayside services not covered by the freight charge or charges on which the shipping line and the transport user have agreed.

4. Availability of tariffs.
Tariffs and related conditions shall be made available on request to transport users at reasonable cost.

5. Notification to the Commission of awards at arbitration and recommendations.
Awards given at arbitration and recommendations made by conciliators that are accepted by the parties shall be notified forthwith to the Commission when they resolve disputes relating to the practices of conferences referred to in Article 4 and in points 2 and 3 above.

In case of a breach of an obligation the Commission may, in order to put an end to such breach, address recommendations or withdraw the block exemption. It may grant an individual exemption according to Article 11 instead. This is laid down in Article 7 of the regulation. The second paragraph of Article 7 gives a detailed procedure for revoking the block exemption when the conditions for granting an exemption are no longer fulfilled. According to Article 7, paragraph 2, under b. special cirumstances are, *inter alia*, created by:

i. acts of conferences or a change of market conditions in a given trade resulting in the absence of elimination of actual or potential competition such as restrictive practices whereby the trade is not available to competition; or

ii. an act of conference which may prevent technical or economic progress or user participation in the benefits;

iii. acts of third countries which:
   – prevent the operation of outsiders in a trade,
   – impose unfair tariffs on conference members,

38

– impose arrangements which otherwise impede technical or economic progress (cargo-sharing, limitations on types of vessels).

If actual or potential competition is absent or may be eliminated as a result of action by a third country, the Commission shall, according to paragraph c, under 1, enter into consultations with the competent authorities of the third country concerned, followed if necessary by negotiations under directives to be given by the Council, in order to remedy the situation. In these circumstances the Commission shall withdraw the benefit of the block exemption. It may at the same time decide whether an individual exemption should be granted.

Apart from the block exemption for conferences Article 6 provides for a block exemption for agreements between conferences and shippers. Such agreement may cover rates, conditions and quality of liner services. This block exemption may also be revoked under the grounds provided for in Article 7. Similarly, it may be substituted by an individual exemption. As noted above, Article 9 contains rules for conflicts of international law. It may be that the application of the regulation to certain restrictive practices or clauses may conflict with the provisions laid down by law or regulations of certain third countries which would compromise important Community trading and shipping interests. If that is the case, the Commission shall at its earliest opportunity undertake consultations with the competent authorities of the third countries concerned, aimed at reconciling as far as possible the above mentioned interests with respect to community law. The Commission shall inform the Advisory Committee referred to in Article 15 of the outcome of these consultations. According to the second paragraph the Commission shall make the recommendations to the Council in order to obtain authorization to open the necessary negotiations. The Commission shall conduct these negotiations in consultation with the Advisory Committee.

It should be noted that there is a considerable amount of overlap between the procedure of Articles 9 and 7, paragraph 2. The original proposal only contained Article 9 for dealing with conflicts with international law. The procedure of Article 7, paragraph 2 is the result of the desire to demarcate the block exemption as clearly as possible. It is also the result of a wish to put the flag up to third countries. Revoking the block exemption is the most clear cut instrument of the regulation. It is therefore to be expected that the procedure of Article 7, paragraph 2 will take precedence over the more general procedure of Article 9.

3. Rules of procedure

This section is largely patterned after Regulation 1017/68. A novelty is Article 11, paragraph 4. This provision allows the Commission, when acting on a complaint or on its own initiative, to conclude that an agreement satisfies the provisions of Article 85, paragraph 3. In other words, it allows the Commission to grant an individual exemption without prior notification. Together with the procedure for the application of an exemption under Article 85, paragraph 3, in Article 12, this provision fundamentally changes the usual competition regime such as it is laid down in regulation no. 17.

Article 12 provides for agreements which do not benefit from the block exemption a possibility to obtain an individual exemption. Article 12 embodies an opposition procedure.[14] If there is no opposition the agreement shall be deemed to be exempted for a maximum of 6 years from the date of publication in the Official Journal. The procedure implies that prior notification is not necessary. Justifying this procedure the preamble points to the special characteristic of maritime transport. It is, according to the preamble, primarily the responsibility of undertakings to see to it that their agreements conform to the rules on competition and consequently their notification to the Commission need not be made compulsory. In this context it should be noted that the shipping industry has always been known for its self regulation.

The opposition procedure of Article 12 is similar to that of Regulation 1017/68. It differs from the opposition procedure in recent block exemption regulations relating to patent licenses and research and development agreements. Contrary to the latter procedure, notification is not necessary. A further difference is that under Article 12 the Commission is obliged to publish a summary of the applications in the Official Journal and invite all interested parties and Member States to submit their comments. This difference creates more procedural safeguards than those contained in the recent block exemptions. The first difference, however, creates legal uncertainty. It enables interested parties at all times to go for an individual exemption. The absence of the obligation to notify and the possibility of Article 11, paragraph 4 to apply Article 85, paragraph 3, on the Commission's own initiative, creates a presumption that cartels are not prohibited. This presumption is further strenghtened by the above indicated omission in this regulation concerning the direct applicability of Article 85, paragraph 1.

What should a national court do when during an application for nullification under Article 85, paragraph 2, the defendant applies for an individual exemption under Article 12? The answer should, I submit, be that the court should apply Article 85, paragraph 1 and declare the agreement void. If there is any reason to doubt, the court may raise a preliminary question before the Court in Luxembourg. It may also stay the proceedings and await the outcome of the Commission's decision. There is a fundamental differ-

---

[14] *See* Venit, J.S. The Commission's opposition procedure-between the Scylla of Ultra Vires and the Charybdis of perfume: legal consequences and tactical considerations, [1985] 22 CMLRev. page 167–202.

ence with the common procedure under Regulation no. 17. Under Regulation no. 17, agreements which have not been notified can never qualify for exemption. This enables the application of Article 85, paragraph 2 by national courts. In the absence of such a clear-cut rule, one might even argue along similar lines as the Court employed in the Bosch[15] and the Asjes Case that agreements in the shipping sector enjoy temporary validity. Such an argument may be refuted by stating that the present regulation does apply Articles 85 and 86. The regulation does not specifically disapply Article 85, paragraph 2. Furthermore, it may be noted that contrary to the Bosch and the Asjes Case, the Commission and the defendants have the opportunity to respectively apply Article 85, paragraph 3 or to apply for an exemption. Finally, according to Article 12, paragraph 4, last sentence, the Commission may in its decision give effect to the exemption from a date prior to that of the application. This is the logical consequence of the fact that prior notification is not a necessary condition for the exemption.

4. Conclusion

There are two ways of evaluating the present regulation. From the point of view of the competition lawyer one may note that the present block exemption is stretching things quite far. Especially where the possibility of elimination of competition is concerned the block exemption may defy the conditions of Article 85, paragraph 3. In view of the uncertainty concerning the eliminating of competition it would have been more in line with the general competition policy to go for individual exemptions. It should also be noted that in the course of the negotiations several conditions were transformed into obligations. Thereby of course softening the competition regime considerably. It should further be noted that there is neither a condition nor an obligation relating to currency adjustment factors. Currency adjustment factors are to shipping what monetary compensatory amounts are to agriculture. Furthermore, the provisions concerning loyalty arrangements which are largely in line with the relevant provisions of the Code of Conduct, are not very stringent. In the light of the case law of the Court in judgments such as Hoffmann-La Roche,[16] their legality may be doubted. Such doubt is particularly appropriate in the situation where competition by outsiders is largely absent. Their demotion from conditions to obligations further erodes the legal nature of these provisions.

On the other hand, it may be noted that the Commission has ample

---

[15] Case 13/61, *Kledingverkoopbedrijf de Geus en Uitdenbogerd v. Robert Bosch GmbH*, 6 April 1962, ECR 1962, page 45.

[16] Case 85/76, *Hoffmann-La Roche & Co AG v. Commission* ('Vitamines'), 13 February 1979, ECR 1979, page 461.

powers to intervene in case of non-observance of obligations. A further positive point is the obligation for conferences to offer transport users free choice for inland transport operations and quay-side services.

The serious drawback is the legal uncertainty which is created by the regulation. There is no provision declaring Article 85, paragraph 1 directly applicable. There is no obligation to notify prior to applying for an exemption. Similarly, the power for the Commission to apply Article 85, paragraph 3 in infringement procedures creates the impression that cartels in the shipping industry are generally accepted.

The shipping industry, of course, values matters differently. It feels that the block exemption was necessary because of the adoption of the Code of Conduct for liner conferences. Furthermore the fact that the Code does contain ample regulations for conferences diminishes the necessity for the Community to adopt competition rules. It is, in view of the Code of Conduct, most undesirable that the Commission enacts rules which differ from the rules contained in the Code adopted on a worldwide scale. Furthermore, shipping circles will point out that the position of conferences has recently been increasingly weakened by outside competition. In other words, there should be no fear that outside competition enabling the block exemption is lacking. The shipping industry values the provisions relating to the accommodation of conflicts of international law. The industry is, however, worried that the block exemption may be withdrawn in the absence of ship owners' anticompetitive action, solely because of measures from third countries. The industry also notes with pleasure that contrary to the original proposal from 1981 the present regulation does not embody compulsory notification. That takes away the fear that the European Commission will establish itself as a 'European Maritime Commission'. The regulation contains a well developed set of rules for conflicts of jurisdiction. The Community claims jurisdication for inbound and outbound maritime transport. As a result of this fundamental position the Community may claim jurisdiction in instances where authorities from third countries impair competition. Thus it is possible to counter unilateral actions by third countries. The Community has moved a long way from the traditional laissez faire policy of the countries of Western Europe. That policy has only resulted in negative powers contained in the so-called blocking statutes. The present procedure for resolving international conflicts of enforcement jurisdiction provides for adequate mechanisms. These provisions are also in line with public international law.

The regulation is not only based on Article 87 as its title would suggest, but also on Article 84, paragraph 2. Reason for the latter inclusion is that by embodying procedures for dealing with conflicts of international law the regulation clearly contains elements of shipping policy.

The regulation is very much designed to give rules for conferences. As a result of this the position of outsiders, liner services outside conferences, is underexposed. The block exemption only relates to conferences. Agreements by outsiders have to be judged as a result of individual complaints and by applications for individual exemptions. Yet the condition of Article 4 and the obligations of Article 5 are attached to the block exemption only. They are therefore not applied to outsiders. It will therefore be important that the Commission, when judging individual complaints or applications for exemption, considers the application of the condition and obligations to outsiders.

Contrary to what one would expect, there is no provision for the revoking of Regulation no. 141 as far as it concerns liner transport. Regulation no. 141 should, of course, remain in force for the other sectors of maritime transport.

IV. Competition and Cooperation: An Economic Perspective

H.W. DE JONG

1. Introduction: The market structure focus

Western style capitalism is again going through a turbulent phase. The recession of the early Eighties, which struck the world economy, has withered away. A new expansionary mood has taken hold of the market economies, understandably of different intensity in the various countries. Market economies have large, not to say seemingly endless, numbers of markets for goods, services, resources, rights and firms. Everything is tradeable, between sellers and buyers and the variety would seem to be so large that apparently 'there is no system in the madness'. When everything is in flux and the old cry 'capitalism is change' (Schumpeter) has become trite, what can one say about the ways events are ordered? For the economist this is the perennial question: under what order does society live and work, and what are the welfare outcomes flowing from the changes that are taking place?

European economists of the post-war period, devoting themselves to the study of markets, have learned to distinguish between the process and the structure (or organization) of markets. Classical, Neo-classical and more recently, Neo-Austrian economic theories have focussed their attention mainly on the economic process, be it in a static or in a more dynamic sense. The production and exchange of goods and services, pricing, advertising, innovation and the growth of firms and markets, as well as the strategies of firms are, of course, of prime importance, but so are the ways markets are organized. Market structure has therefore been the focal point of study of so-called industrial organization theorists and the questions they pose themselves were focussed on the way markets are organized and to what effect.

What forms does competition take, how intensive does it work, what about cartels, joint ventures, franchising and other cooperative organizations and, as a third dimension, what level and direction does concentration take and how is it influenced by mergers, take-overs, vertical integration, diversification and conglomerization?

Again, one could approach this structuring and restructuring of markets (and even of whole economies) in a static or in a dynamic sense. The first method was used in the Fifties and Sixties to find out whether particular market structures are conducive to better economic performance, as mea-

45

sured by the level of profit rates, price flexibility and (sometimes) economic progress. But, increasingly, the dynamic approach gained in importance, because it came to be realized that market structures themselves are liable to change, mainly under the influence of the actors in the field and their behaviour. And so structure and process came to be theoretically intertwined into a complex, interwoven fabric constantly being reworked by the principal players, that is business firms. During the Seventies and Eighties two extra dimensions were added: the international, border-crossing aspect as manifest in the rise of multinationalization and the policy aspect, as governments started to interfere in markets by means of competition, trade, and industrial policies.

2. The competitive cycle

The core concepts which are used in the new industrial organization theory (or market theory as it is called in continental Europe) are competition, cooperation and control. They represent organizational forms used by firms in markets to organize the processes of production, exchange, investment and innovation, pricing, etc. to their own advantage; i.e. they are used by firms to strengthen their relative positions in the markets in which they operate, and that may cover penetration and expansion as well as withdrawal.

Competition is rivalry between firms, taking place under conditions of uncertainty. In the competitive process there are 'given', such as products, processes, rules, customs and traditions, but no one can bank upon them. They may be changed by innovatory products and modes of behaviour from the side of market participants, and if these are more efficient than the previous ways of doing things the latter will be superseded.

This innovative function of competition, is joined by the allocative function under which productive resources are shifted from the less valuable applications to the more valuable uses. Allocation and reallocation serve the creation of wealth but assume flexibility in the use of the means of production and of the institutional scaffolding of the economy.

Both competitive functions are not subject to the rules of a normal sporting game, to which economic competition is often likened. The latter, if one wants to draw the comparison, is more like the Palio horse contest, held in summer months in Siena, Tuscany, in which the City's communities may tempt drivers and horses away from rival communities before the game starts, may make alliances and undo them, and in which, apart from alertness and efficiency, power may be called into the 'game'. Also, there are real victims among men and horses, quite unlike in normal sporting games.

Furthermore, competitive rivalry is between unequals who have differing aims and means. This is unlike the parties in the perfectly competitive

46

model, who have similar goals, equal means and show like behaviour. Competitive rivalry is more or less as farm production used to be organized in former days when farmers were supposed to compete, but did not feel like being competitors.

Uncertainty is therefore the hallmark of competition and is in its turn, enhanced by competitive rivalry. It must be shouldered in real markets by someone who is prepared to contract resources (labour, capital, means of transport, etc.) before production starts at fixed prices and sell the output at uncertain prices. This facing of uncertainty, interposed between ex-ante fixed commitments and ex-post outcomes, qualifies the entrepreneur. The facing of uncertainty, however is a necessary, not a sufficient condition of entrepreneurship. For, on the one hand, an entrepreneur may take the wrong decisions when facing the uncertainties related to the competitive process. Then losses will result and the firm will disappear or will have to be reorganized. On the other hand, the tackling of uncertainty in customary, predictable ways will not be enough to create added value (i.e. a surplus of output value over input value), which is a requirement for the continued existence and growth of firms. To meet these requirements some measure of innovation in the firm's products, production or distribution processes or the ways it organizes its productive resources is necessary. Only such innovations can put the firm ahead of its competitors by creating an advantage they cannot match. Innovations can be large or small, may be revolutionary or just improve upon something existing already, may be difficult to imitate or be easily taken over by some competitor(s). However that may be – and there are obviously enormous differences between branches and time periods as well as between countries in this respect –, uncertainty and innovation are at the basis of the firms' value-creating activity, which results in profits.

The firm which undertakes both activities and scores some measure of succes in achieving surplus value is sooner or later confronted with the imitation and emulation of competitors. The first is the copying and taking over of the innovative move through which the profits melt away. The second is the competition which supplants the original innovation by a move which fulfils the function in a superior way. The better mousetrap supplants the previous one, and in turn is copied itself. Both imitation and emulation can bring in profits, but ultimately, close the circuit: when they have been carried on to the end, the profits will have gone, either because, through imitation, the firm's output value will be reduced to the input value of its resources or, through emulation it will fall below the level of the input value. In order to start the surplus value generating process anew, the firm will need a structural adaptation to qualify it for a continued taking part in the market process. Such structural adaptation may consist in a reshuffling of resources, the adoption of a new management, or a new organization as well as a reorganization of distribution channels, the creation or redirection of research and development and similar measures. The perpetuous follow-

47

Figure 1.   The competitive cycle

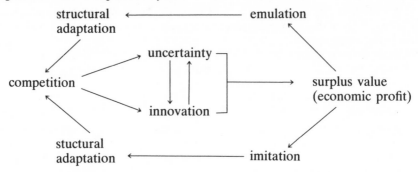

up of these activities, which pertain as well to firms as to groups of firms, constituting so-called branches or sectors of industry, can be represented by the diagram in figure 1.

The figure highlights the inner-workings of the market economy as a never ending process of surplus value creation by means of innovation and uncertainty shouldering. In turn, imitation and emulation compete the profits away, necessitating restructuring in order to qualify for renewed competition. It will be seen that all the terms given in the schema are elements of the entrepreneurial function which is the pivot in the market economy. As Cantillon (1697–1734), a French-Irish banker and economist wrote in his book 'Essai sur la nature du commerce en général (1755)': The production and exchange of goods and services are put in motion and brought forward in Europe by entrepreneurs and, to be sure hazardously.

3.   The organizational principles

Obviously, in most markets there are both uncertainties and innovations, if only because innovations increase uncertainty, and, in reverse, existing uncertainty, especially if becoming large, inspires to the introduction of innovations, both in products and processes. As to the latter, think of the standardization of goods often in conjunction with a given quality which may benefit both the consumer, by reducing his uncertainty as to the variance of qualities offered, and the producer, by permitting him mass-production at reduced unit costs. The brand or trade-mark is a prominent method by which the elimination or reduction of uncertainty is achieved; the values of such names, brands or trade-marks can be very high and enduring and quite a lot of advertising is linked up with its creation and preservation.

The competitive process, as pictured in figure 1, is therefore made up of three main parts:

48

First, there are the thrusts or pushes by firms towards the creation of surplus value through innovations or the meeting of uncertainty. Surplus value is the result of lower costs, given the price; or of higher value, given the costs. The means of action used by competitors are price, quality, service, advertising, and substitution. These are the socalled action parameters of actual competition, that is the rivalry between existing suppliers who are already in the relevant market. Potential competition is the competitive force emanating from suppliers who are not yet in the relevant market, but may become suppliers. Thus they have the potential, which acts as a threat. Three categories of the latter are the firms who may extend their market, or who may add to their product ranges through own production or merger (take-over), and through new firm foundation in the relevant market. Economists are debating the effectiveness of the various means of competitive action, though there is more or less agreement that price and quality competition are of general importance. Newer theories (e.g. Contestable market theory) claim that potential competition is a practical substitute of actual competition, but this claim is theoretically overrated and empirically not strong. Potential competition can hardly serve as a substitute for actual competition.

Second, these surplus values are the challenge to other market suppliers, either to imitate or to emulate the first moves, with the aim to capture the whole or part of the surplus values. By doing this, these reacting firms seek to serve their own interests, but at the same time, when successful, serve society at large. They generalize the innovations and the uncertainty reductions, extend the value creation and, in the process, reduce costs, prices and uncertainties for consumers. The welfare creation of the competitive process is therefore the big trump card of the free market economy, and there is no substitute able to achieve similar gains. To use a metaphor: the competitive machinery of pushes and reactionary moves is unsurpassable because of its compelling force, its broadness of application and the fastness with which it works. No planning authority or committee or negotiating body can substitute for competition in these respects. If such bodies can do what competition does in one respect, e.g. act with compelling authority, they cannot simultaneously fulfil the task in the other respects. Competition, as Marx rightly noted, subdues the competitors and forces them more effectively into the mold of welfare creation than human fiat. It is not only experience which teaches us that planned societies or guided economies lag in welfare creation; the logical argument is that whereas economic agents can argue with planning or regulating human beings, and in so doing can change the conditions, terms or timing of the pushing or reacting moves, one cannot argue with the competitive market. Competition, as long as it exists, uses the method of the fait accompli: and, in the market place, unlike the university or the parliamentary debating room, facts are more effective than arguments.

The *third* part of the competitive process, pictured in figure 1 are the restructurings of firms, operating in the relevant market. The counter attacks, implied in imitative or emulative behaviour of rival companies force the existing firms to reorganize themselves, either through internal adaptation or by forging external links with other firms. Internal adaptation aims at the achievement of a new organizational structure, such that better products, lower production costs, improved quality, service or more intensive advertising are possible to meet the challenges. The reallocation of personnel, financial means or material assets inside the company are required to this end; such measures may be joined by external regroupings, leading up – as is nowaday the case – to divestitures, mergers, take-overs, joint ventures, or other types of inter-firm agreements. All such forms of combination have in common that participating firms combine their resources or behaviour for achieving a shared goal. The structural adaptations required may range through the whole spectrum, from very loose, implicit collusion to well organized, independent firms set up under a joint-venture agreement, sales syndicate or full fledged merger.

I exclude mergers, take-overs and other structures controlling the adhering firms from above from the concept of co-operation; though the demarcation lines between co-operation and control are fluid – as they are between these organizational forms and competition. Control is the organizational form in which decision power is centralized; the firms belonging to the group are no longer independent, though they may have a large measure of operational freedom.

The hallmark of co-operation is an (implicit or explicit) agreement between independent firms to strive for a common goal. The agreement is mostly based on free decision, but in several cases, the firms involved may well feel constrained or compelled to co-operate. The penalty is a reduction of profits or operation at a loss. Suppose a retailer is threatened by price cuts in one of his products from a discounter – with whom he shares the market; he may meet the cut by reducing his own price too and, if the price war proceeds, both competitors may reach an understanding to stop the practice. He may also retaliate by cutting the price of one of the discounter's very profitable goods, and the competitor, perceiving the signal, may stop the price cutting action. In the economist's parlance, both types of behaviour by the rival firms are co-operation, though they bear different names: cartel versus collusion or concerted practice, as Article 85(1) EEC has it.

Co-operation may be defensively or offensively oriented. In the first example the defensive nature of an agreement is apparent: both firms want to end the price cutting. But suppose that during the talks of both retailers there crops up the idea to join forces in a mutually shared enterprise in some other market or to open a shop in some other line of goods where both firms would be in a minority position, we have an example of an offensively oriented co-operation. The difference between the two types is that whereas

50

the first one stops the competitive cycle, as pictured in figure 1, the second one ushers in a new cycle. The meaning of co-operation is also visible from the examples; in the one case, the co-operation leads up to the control of the market, in the other the co-operation intensifies the competition in the other market area or market segment. Therefore, whether co-operation between firms means control or further competition depends on their market shares and the goals of their behaviour. Close reading of Articles 85 and 86 of the EEC Treaty make clear that the economic reasoning outlined above stamps the philosophy of the Community's competition policy. Structural adaptations, be it in the form of cartel agreements, concerted practices or mergers/take-overs or joint ventures and similar forms are acceptable and compatible with the operation of a common market, as long as they do not impair the competitive process.

4.   Conditions determining competition and co-operation

This is the principle, and, pithily it expresses that the European Economic Community has opted for the competitive ordering of the market process. Both co-operation and control, very often worthwhile in themselves and aiming at desireable goals for both the partners and the community at large, find their limits in the persistence of competition. This set-up expresses the Treaty's belief that economic theory is justified in attributing to competition superiority in wealth creation over public or private planning.

Do we need the statement of such a principle and if so, the policy measures designed for effectuating it? The question is important, for, it has been argued in recent years by some schools of economic thinking, that both are largely superfluous: competition can take care of itself. It is argued that competition cannot be suppressed by the co-operative or controlling actions of firms in markets, at least in the somewhat longer run. Hence, competition policy is largely superfluous. However, the argument is not correct. First, we know from economic history that there were in the past enduring monopolies and cartels and it is not reasonable to expect that such events could not occur again. Examples like the Rhenisch Westphalian Coal Syndicate, which lasted some half century or the De Beer's diamond syndicate, existing since the thirties could be multiplied both on the national and international levels.

Second, the degree of competition or the intensity of competition is not a given, but reflects more a continuity, varying from high to low. There are quite a number of circumstances influencing the intensity of competition, such as market share and the distribution thereof, number of competitors, the current and prospective growth rate of the market, the structure of the buyers market, ease of entry, the financial power of parties concerned, etc. These aspects have to be taken into account, for, much as it is true that an economic power position – based on co-operation or control – may be undermined by competitive action, the reverse also holds: power may nullify

51

competition. Suppose our two retailers undertake both actions, that is conclude in the original market a price-raising cartel, and use the profits earned to penetrate another market, with the aim to play a similar game there. It then depends on the circumstances mentioned whether they will succeed, and partly, their enhanced economic power may have a hand there in. They could put pressure on the community's authorities to refuse the establishment of competing retailers or conclude an exclusionary agreement with the property owners in some strategically located shopping area; they might agree with large retailers in another market area to keep out of their market in exchange for their abstinence, etc. (these examples are based on real-life cases in Dutch retailing).

Third, even if an established power position is ultimately contested and competed away, the time period during which the power position has existed is all important. The extra profits earned in this way may well be sufficient to fortify the dominant firm's or group's position and provide it with the means to further distort the competitive process.

This dialectical relationship between the organization principles of a market economy makes it necessary to review the requirements for their operation.

Economists study the conditions influencing competition and co-operation and group them into variables, as depicted by figure 2.

Figure 2.

Co-operation (collusion) or control promoting variables	*Competition promoting variables*
• Asymmetrical size relationships between firms	Symmetrical size relationships between firms
• Tight oligopoly or numerous firms	Wide oligopoly
• Homogeneous product or service	Heterogeneous product or service
• Stagnating market growth	Dynamic market expansion (a.o. based on innovations)
• Identical cost functions	Diverging cost functions
• Capital intensive production and high overhead costs	Overcapacity
• Conservative business mentality	Aggressive behaviour by at least one party
• Uncertainty reducing information, available to all partners	Appropriable knowledge

The left hand column in the figure may give rise either to co-operative behaviour or to control. The one may also shade over into the other if it does become clear that co-operative behaviour yields inferior results compared to control.

52

For example, cartels have been found to be a substitute for outright mergers, but they were also, in many cases, the prelude to the formation of control organizations in which decision power was centralized in a few hands. It is therefore not correct to sustain the view that co-operation between firms prevents an otherwise unavoidable concentration movement (W. Benisch, 1982); that depends very much on a number of circumstances.

Two inferences may be deduced from figure 2:

First, the best set of conditions promoting competition can be summarized as a wide, symmetrical, heterogeneous oligopoly in a growing market where knowledge can and will be appropriated and contested. Such a market structure promotes price and quality competition, which will be visible also from a continous shift of rank positions as measured by differencies in market shares (the so-called fluidity-index, De Jong 1987). In contrast, asymmetrical, tight oligopolies in stagnating, homogenous markets, where information is shared by competitors preserves the *status quo* and inspires a conservationist attitude among business leaders. Both extremes are visible in some branches of industry (compare European cement production or the US automobile market structure with, for example, the world's personal computer market), though most sectors show some mix-up of competitive and co-operative elements. The balance may change over time too, especially when market growth gives way to stagnant conditions.

Second, competition and co-operation are not only alternatives, as was stated earlier, but may also be complementary. That is, firms may compete to force a co-operation or control, as is evident from many contested mergers or take overs. In reverse, a co-operative attitude may be used temporarily to continue the rivalry later on. Shakespeare shows this with unsurpassable insight, when, in 'The taming of the shrew', he has Hortensio and Gremio, being rivals for Bianca's hand, co-operate in helping her wild, older sister to a husband first before setting forth the competition, because the father of both girls insists on the marriage of the younger one after that of the older. Thus, consenting on the prematureness of action they are even prepared to pay for the costs of removing the obstacle on their road: 'and would I had given him the best horse in Padua to begin his wooing...'

5. Co-operation and its varieties

Co-operation between firms may, as we have seen, cover a wide field and relate to agreements, concerted practices: or institutionalized forms, such as joint ventures, and franchising systems.

The best approach is to make a distinction between co-operation of small and medium sized businesses and that of large firms. There has been a tendency, both in the United States and in Europe to make room for more

53

co-operation between firms; this is visible in the areas where co-operation is permitted, the forms which are found acceptable and (in the United States) in the reduced penalties placed on tresspassing the rules. The social pressures to allow for more co-operation come from various corners, which can best be dealt with in the context of small versus large business.

During the late Seventies and early Eighties there took place a change in appreciation in Western societies with respect to small business. Economic research found out that small and medium sized businesses were far from negligible contributors to the innovation process, in particular in so far as the myriad of small improvements and the finding of important, not too costly, inventions are concerned. Moreover, small businesses have been found to be important creators of employment, not only for the owners who started them, but also for extending this employment to salaried employees. In nearly all countries of the OECD small business gained in employment, whereas big business (the top 500 or 1,000 largest firms) has lost employment.

Third, the Japanese example underlined tendencies present also in other countries that small business serves an important function as supplier of components, parts and specialist functions and as a distributor of the goods of large-scale firms.

These experiences have led to measures to reinforce the position of small businesses in the market. Such measures generally were taken with the aims:

 a. to compensate for the disadvantages small businesses have when competing,
 b. to reinforce their competitive power over and against the big firms,
 c. to facilitate the taking up of production and/or distribution and thus to create employment,
 d. to promote innovation, by means of facilitating R & D efforts.

In reverse, large firms have had their problems too, consisting of the necessity to face much stronger international competition, to cope with the technological revolutions occurring in informatics, biotechnology, space and new materials.

As the problems were not the same for these two categories, the measures had to be differentiated too. The EC Commission used the following criteria to distinguish the two groups: market share and absolute sales and has, additionally in a number of cases, also used a time limit for allowing co-operation. The Authorities in the United States, have with a view to the supposed international competitive threat for large firms and the bright development of small firms in that country, mainly eased co-operation between large firms.

Let us quickly review these developments, in so far as they relate to competition policy matters (fiscal and other types of measures are not dealt with here).

54

In the EC, the Commission has:

- freed specialization agreements, especially those between small and medium sized businesses, from the prohibition of Art. 85(1) if the group's market share is not larger than 20% and total sales of all firms is not more than 500 million ECU. If the sales limit is surpassed, a new six month procedure can be started.
- Exclusive dealings have been set free in 1983 when sales of one of the partners was no more than 100 million ECU, and in 1984 for exclusive buying when sales did not go beyond 100 million ECU and the time for the agreement was not more than 5 years (10 years for beer brewery and petrol station contracts): Measures were also taken with respect to exclusive and selective clauses in motor car distribution contracts in 1985.
- Small business cartels were considered in a policy statement as of September 1986 to be compatible with the competition rules in so far as their market share is less than 5% and the combined sales of the cartellized firms less than 200 million ECU.
- Research and development agreements in so far as concluded between non-competing firms were exempted for a period of 5 years starting with the first sale of the products. Co-operations between competitors were exempted from the prohibition of Art. 85(1) if the sales of the goods did not reach a market share of over 20%. If, after 5 years, the 20% limit is surpassed a new exemption will only be exceptionally given,
- to ease the transfer of technical knowledge and improve the competitive position of European industry, bilateral agreements between two firms relating to licensing of patents and technical knowledge were freed in so far as they assumed stipulated conditions.
- policy with respect to joint ventures is in the making, but a preview by Mr Sutherland has let it be known that quantitative criteria will here be decisive too: a market share of between 15 and 20% will evoke scrutiny; of over 20%, will bring a prohibition of the joint venture,
- franchising systems are part of the exclusive distribution arrangements, exempted by category, but, being systems with distinctive traits, linked up with the identity and goodwill of the franchise giver, have to be dealt with separately.

The reason is that franchise systems have, more than simple co-operations, also control elements, which make the clash with effective competition more of a reality. Such control elements are vertical price fixation, the prohibition of sales to other franchise takers and the division of territories. Again, in the Yves Rocher case of 1986, a quantitative criterion (market share of 5%, maximum total sales) was used to measure the importance of the element of territorial division.

In the United States,

- export cartels were given more freedom in 1985 (Guidelines relating to Export Trading Company Immunity) than they already had under the Webb-Pomerene Act of 1918 and the Export Trading Company Act of 1982.
- Research and development agreements between firms (including large ones) were freed from the *per se* prohibition and brought under a rule of reason in the National Co-operative Research Act of 1984. Moreover, treble damage suits were abolished as a possibility, as was also the case with export cartels which tresspass the Anti-trust laws.
- In 1983 the Department of Justice for the first time applied Anti-trust immunity to small business co-operation which was contained in section 9(d) of the Small Business Act of 1958, but which had never been honoured.

Summarizing the European experience with respect to co-operative agreements one might conclude that social and economic developments have pushed co-operation between firms to a more prominent place in the organizational scale of business. However, it was recognized that co-operation (like control) between firms can be used both to stimulate as well as to block or impair competition, and the primacy of competition as a means to achieve surplus value and to diffuse it throughout society was retained. In other words, it has been recognized that co-operation is not a neutral principle, which can safely be left in the hands of participants; still less, that co-operation is a way of organizing relationships between firms which is better than and should take precedence over competition, a theory often advanced by business spokesmen.

6. Advantages and dis-advantages of co-operation

This brings us to the question whether the business point of view is without economic merit. If the existence of numerous, independent business firms was considered to be the hallmark of competition as some economists think, then all types of co-operation should be prohibited. For, either such co-operations would already imply a reduction of competition if they would be the initial steps leading up to that goal. Such reasoning would fit in with the interpretation of Article 85(1) by some lawyers that all agreements between firms reduce competition, because an agreement to unify behaviour necessarily reduces the number of independent competitors which is equivalent to diminished competition. The analytical weakness of this argument was already exposed in previous debates, however. Competition is not a numbers game; it consists of the dynamic procedure, under which firms create advantages which can be contested and competed away. This is visible in nearly every market where differentiated products and services appear appealing to consumers in general or to particular segments of them. In this way innovations and product differentiations (e.g. by means of higher qual-

56

ities, or brands or trade names) develop specialized markets, which initially are rather narrow and distinguished from the prevalent general run of products. The processes of imitation and emulation broaden subsequently the area of competition until the initial feature is generally applied. This is the way in which motor car improvements like power steering, electronic ignition, safety cages and other technical devices and designs were incorporated into the industry's products. Alongside price competition, imitation and emulation are part and parcel of the competition process.

It is similar with organizational or structural adaptations. Co-operational devices may also have some major advantages at this stage, such as

1) The possibility to take on complex transactions, where individual competition does not work or very imperfectly. Either the transactions are too large for even very big firms or they are too many-sided, so that firms with varying expertise need to collaborate for achieving worthwhile results. Drilling for oil at sea, deep sea mining, aero space ventures, etc. are prominent examples. There, large scale and complex transactions are the basis for contractual joint ventures (also called consortia) and equity joint ventures, where a separate company is founded. Producer co-operatives, in the agricultured sphere, are also in this category; a separate firm is established to process the sugar beets or the raw milk from farmers, because the latter are unable individually to realize the necessary economies of scale in production and marketing and are not qualified to develop the specialized knowledge, upon which a processing plant can be founded.

2) Cooperation often serves a useful goal by correcting an otherwise weak market position. That is, they create some countervailing power, as was apparent in consumer co-operatives *vis-à-vis* powerful suppliers of goods, or producer and purchasing co-operatives *vis-à-vis* suppliers and competitors. Joint ventures likewise, are sometimes set up to correct an otherwise weak market position of the individual participants. What is a virtue may sometimes be changed over into a vice, however. Co-operative power positions may well turn out to be as anti-competitive as private dominant positions, as the recent Meldoc case illustrates, and joint ventures may be used to close a market, to raise entrance barriers, or to function as a cloak for sharing the pains of retreat where a crisis cartel would not find favour.

3) Co-operation between firms may be required to take up new activities which involve high risks, because of the unique uncertainties linked up with them, that only a group of firms can cope with these. The firms share the risks and distribute the burdens in accordance with their shouldering capacity, willingness to take risks, past experience in handling new activities, and other factors. This is perhaps the most difficult category for an outsider to judge on its merits: does co-operation really mean to promote the new activities, or is it a pretended organization for warding off and blocking

57

foreign competitors, put pressure for funds on national or international authorities, and so on. As we have seen, one of the two main pressures for intensified co-operation, and especially that between large firms, is in this area.

The last point raises a problem of general importance: should a co-operative agreement between firms be allowed if the co-operation achieves a number of advantages (real, not pretended) even if the intensity of competition is being reduced, for example, if some leading competitors within the common market by means of joining forces can better compete against non – EC firms? Industrial circles have often advocated this point of view; they are nowadays seconded by US authorities, who argue that international competition requires the attenuation of the Anti-trust laws.

Essentially, the argument is about a rule of reason for co-operative agreements, under which a net balance of the advantages of co-operation and the disadvantages of reduced competition should be established. Article 85(1) does not allow for such a balancing act. The grant of an exemption by virtue of Article 85(3) requires, however, the maintenance of competition, in respect of a substantial part of the products in question: One could logically infer that co-operation limiting competition in an non-nessential part of the market is tolerable.

The Commission has quantified this as we have seen earlier; such a setting of numerical limits has been questioned a. o. with the argument that a fixed percentage (say 15% market share) may be sometimes too high and sometimes too low, depending on the distribution of economic power on both the supply and the demand side of the market (Benisch 1982, p. 412–414). That may be true analytically, but politically such a 'fine-tuning' of the rules severely complicates the procedures and increases the burdens of the supervising authority. It also entails the danger of sliding rules, because economic power cannot be measured ordinally, but at best only cardinally (that is, not in absolute numbers, but only relatively to each other). Thus Art. 85(3) is not a rule of reason; it only says that co-operative agreements between firms which raise productivity and benefit the consumer are allowed if they do not impair competition; if they do, they stand condemned. Again, this line of reasoning is in accordance with good economic theory which holds, that in a large market, fierce internal competition promotes external strength. Finally, it is well to keep in mind that many co-operative agreements fail to reach their goal. This is so, because co-operation is a half-way house: it binds firms in some respects, but leaves them free to cancel the agreement. This entails the 'paradox of co-operation', which says that the result of the co-operation has to be ascribed as well to the collaboration as to the participating firms individually.

An independent firm, realizing this knows that it cannot be compelled to do additional things, often essential for the success of the co-operative action. It may even try to change the terms of the agreement, if it knows that its co-operation is necessary. With that aim in mind it may build up its

58

position inside the group and force subsequently the terms in its favour. Finally, it may 'cheat' on the co-operation's rules or articles of agreement.

Most co-operative organizations – at least the horizontal ones – are therefore weak and unstable. They are dissolved, have to be reorganized or loose out in the market contest after sometime. Examples can be abundantly found in the litterature relating to cartels (Lenel 1970), joint ventures (Hoekman 1984 and De Jong, 1987), joint purchasing organizations, etc. Let me illustrate again with an example from retailing. The so-called free co-operative chains of retailers (of which Spar is a well-known example in Europe) have lost market share to the large retail chains in several European countries. In the Netherlands their decline went from some 30% in 1970 to less than 18% in the middle eighties. The main reasons were:

1) The co-operative chain shops are thinly spread throughout the country and have starkly differing sizes of shops. Both factors put them at a disadvantage in marketing effectiveness and transport costs within the organization, in comparison with regional and national retail chains. In the latter cases, the top management may induce efficiency, which is impossible in the co-operative chains.

2) Co-operative chains have problems in gaining access to shopping areas, to which the purchasing power shifted in past decades, have limited financial means (again the independence of retailers!) and often have problems of collaboration.

3) Countervailing power against (large scale) suppliers of branded articles was stronger in centralized retail chains, who also were more flexible and innovative in introducing their own brands than co-operative chains.

Likewise, so-called shared joint-ventures have been less effective than dominant parent ventures (in which one of the parents takes managerial control, in contrast to shared management responsibility), while, in addition, the shared joint ventures operated less satisfactoraly when the balance of parents' responsibility was more equal than when it was largely unbalanced (Killing 1983, p. 22–29).

In cartels, the productivity performance and the adaptation to changed circumstances is often less, than in large corporations, depending on the degree of organization and the distribution of power within the cartel.

7. Conclusion

It is therefore not true that co-operative activity is better than either competition or control, as excercized by large organizations. Co-operation is often only a palliative to these, agreed upon because firms want to keep their independence in future and be free to abandon the group when it suits their purposes. While one may agree with their evolution as long as they do not impair competition in the market, they certainly should not be artificially promoted by the Authorities, or be allowed to creep up the sleeves of European competition policy.

References

W. Benisch (1982), Kooperationserleichterungen und Wettbewerb, in: Cox, Jens and Market, Handbuch des Wettbewerbs, München.

J.M. Hoekman (1984), The role of the joint venture in the strategy of corporations, Amsterdam.

H.W. de Jong (1985), Dynamische markttheorie, Leiden.

H.W. de Jong (1987), Market structures in the European Economic Community, in: Mays and van Veen, European integration and industry, Tilburg.

J.P. Killing (1983), Strategies for joint venture success, London and Canberra.

H.O. Lenel (1970), Die Problematik der Kartelle und Syndikate, in: Arndt(ed.). Die Konzentration in der Wirtschaft, Berlin.

I. Schmidt (1987), Wettbewerbspolitik und Kartellrecht, Stuttgart.

V.   Intra-enterprise co-operation, geographical price discrimination and the disunion of the 'internal' market

H. W<small>ITLOX</small>

> *Let him who is without sin among you cast the first stone*
>
> *John 7.53*

1.   Introduction

A present overriding aim of the Member States of the European Economic Community is to produce a single internal market – whatever the distinction between 'internal' and the classic 'common' may be.

Articles 85 and 86 of the EEC Treaty provide business firms with the main and most solid buttress of European economic unity. The Sherman Act and the other American antitrust laws, the Gesetz gegen Wettbewerbsbeschränkung in Germany and the laws of the other Member States in the field of competition can assume that unity exists. They can, consequently, concentrate on pure competition problems as the economists and lawyers of the country concerned see them. But the task set to the European Commission by the Articles 85 and 86 is not so much to formulate an all-embracing competition policy but to help create the unity of a market. Competition policy is in the first instance a tool for unity.

The phenomenon of 'price' has here a central place. As elderly economists put it: the price is a thermometer for what happens on the market-place, but it is also a thermostat indicating impossibilities and possibilities, provoking mobility. In the nature of things this is only valid for prices which have found their equilibrium level under the pressure of effective market forces. Individually or collectively 'administered' prices respond to artificial elements not in accordance with the requirements of the open market economy aimed at by the EEC Treaty. *Per definitionem* 'guided' prices for products put on the market by undertakings combined in a formal cartel, in an oligopoly – inevitable in most modern branches of industry and so to be considered the rule – or by firms in a dominant position should therefore be looked at with particular circumspection by those who are entrusted by the consumer and taxpayer with the progressive realization of the unity of the Common Market.

The unity of the Common Market is for undertakings a problem of profitability, not a matter of principle but of pence. Artificial price-fixing will therefore be realized, formally or not, as long as it is remunerative – after deduction of any fines: until today, and in the light of the decisions and court rulings price-fixing systems do not seem to have been considered by the Commission as striking at the core of the Common Market. Nevertheless many publicly known pricing practices and systems are very effective instruments for maintaining the partitioning of the desired unity of the common market into traditional national markets. Here is still a largely unexplored field where the productivity of any effort will be tremendously great. There are in the Common Market too many conventional price-fixers. Every victory of the Commission weakens the efficiency of undetected collusions. So, the bringing of some strategic cases against typical nationalistic practices seems strongly desirable.

To avoid any misinterpretation of what will follow it should be mentioned that the author is an economist, initially active in industry and then for almost 30 years in the price- and competition departments of the ECSC and the EEC. As an economist he had the occasion to appreciate the often rather tangential approach to unity and competition problems under the Treaty of Rome. 'Peripheral' matters such as clauses concerning exclusivity in distribution contracts, specialisation, research are not the heart of the matter, but the prices for the suppliers and distributors resulting from the contracts in question: it is always the price which is the crucial preoccupation of the parties concerned. The exclusivity contracts for example are only devices to maximize profits. To do so is the right of any firm, small or large. However, bigger under-takings succeed in doing this without any 'peripheral' measure. As where they have dominant power or are one of the happy few in the branch and so can arrange things informally, they are able to realize supra-optimal price-levels without any formal help from other colleagues.

I have chosen two situations to illustrate these price practices that undermine the unity of the Common Market. The first concerns the overall sales policy applied by transnational groups, the second concerns a specific form of price fixing. The basic facts turn on facts which I could sum up by three questions:

– Modern manufactured products for mass consumption such as records, foodstuffs, medicines, films, lamps, electrical apparatus, even if produced in only one or two factories, have in most cases – after deduction of taxes – different wholesale prices in the Member States. In terms of what criteria do manufacturing groups determine these prices and how are they maintained? Is it a matter of discrimination between national markets?

62

- Homogeneous industrial basic products – like metals, glass, fertilizers, building materials – are often sold at c.i.f. prices which are uniform within each Member State or specific geographical price zones. In such a situation not only do buyers near the factory subsidize buyers at greater distance as they pay a part of the latter's transport costs but the seller also differentiates according to the nationality of the buyer. Is this practice not discriminatory?
- 'Transnational' c.i.f. or delivered pricelists are nearly non-existent in case of exports. The delivered prices of the leading manufacturer of the country of destination is followed. What remains of the Common Market in this situation?

These are just examples of critical situations which until now have had no explicit place in the EEC jurisprudence. Pricing practices play a crucial role, however, in the realization of an open 'internal' market. The necessity of such a market has in recent years been stressed particularly by the leaders of the big transnational groups. It will be shown that also these groups have to do their duty in this respect. They should stop using commercial instruments which surely make their position comfortable – *divide et impera!* – but which are clearly anti-Common Market.

2. Cartels versus intra-enterprise co-operation

A. The working of the transnational group

Let us consider first the practices of transnational groups.

Inter-enterprise co-operation falls by definition under Article 85 of the EEC Treaty. On the other hand doctrine and the case law are unclear – to say the least – about intra-enterprise co-operation. Mostly it is supposed that intra-enterprise co-operation within transnational groups cannot exist, as there is no independent individuality of the members of the group. Such a verdict grants a degree of permissiveness to transnational corporations which is forbidden for smaller ones. However, the phenomenon of intra-group activities has a specific EEC dimension as these can, and often so, hamper the unity of the Common Market. In the centre is the commercial activity of the big transnational corporations.

These groups of firms possess concentrated power of sufficient quantity and quality in many countries to offer a base for the application of anti-competitive market-partitioning tactics. I do not go as far as e.g. the economist Galbraith or the historian Braudel who, more or less accusingly, state that the laws of the market no longer exist for the modern capitalist corporations and that only smaller and medium sized firms are still subject to them. It is too difficult to eliminate 'the' market totally and competition between the economic giants often happens to be very strong indeed, what-

63

ever they may invent to eliminate market forces and guide the supply and demand curves in their direction. I observe that for the purpose of this article, I take the transnational groups *sine ira et studio* – without antipathy or sympathy. I just want to point to some aspects of their way of life in the light of the morality defined in the Treaty of Rome and in the White Paper of 1985 concerning the completion of the internal market. Feeling – *mutatis mutandis!* – a little bit like Virgil Walling with, and trying to guide Dante in the Purgatorio and surely not like Beatrice guiding him in the Paradiso!...

It is natural and their duty that public authorities, individuals and corporations always try, with different means, to organize the assets subject to their control so as to maximize profits. Here the modern capitalist diversified and transnational group has special facilities of a geographic nature: its powerful and very personalized presence on different geographic – i.a. national – markets provides the possibility to create, alone or in oligopolistic concertation with others, spatial sub-markets. 'Divide et impera' is often a profitable 'Leitmotiv'. So the transnational groups can have a decisive impact on the unity of the Common Market through their affiliates which have a vocation which is defined in national-geographic terms. This impact is as great as – and surely more effective than the impact of formal cartels between undertakings of a more modest size.

The reader of the rare Commission decisions and Court rulings defining some norms for transnational aggregate enterprises – needless to mention them – will, however, find a discrepancy between the existing legal doctrine concerning the quasi-impossibility of any risk to the unity of the Common Market produced by intra-group arrangements and the omnipresence of harmful effects of collective, cartel-like market sharing by minor undertakings. Comparable, not to say economically identical situations are treated with different measures, dependent on the origin of the restrictive situation or practice. Independent undertakings united in a cartel or a cartel-like structure and of a group of firms, a trust or a 'Konzern' doing the same as a cartel but under the guidance of a well structured diversified decision centre of transnational character are until now assessed differently.

I am convinced that this disequilibrium of treatment has to be attributed to a dominating legalistic approach to competition problems in the Common Market. Exaggerating: a contract can be submitted to desk-analysis, a difference in the net prices applied on e.g. the French and German markets may not, if a cartel produces different prices in the different member countries – which possibly means price discrimination – the point of departure can be found in the basic agreement. If a transnational group does the same, the point of departure is a probably informal decision at the headquarters, national permissiveness for the affiliates with home market protection, and concertation with the other affiliates of the group and with competitors (price leadership!). If one observes a substantial price difference for a given product between the different Member States for a long period, this should be considered as a proof of the presence of sand in the driving gear of the

64

Common Market. Commercial facts like price-lists, rebates, transport conditions, are as, and often more important than contracts in identifying the existence or the non-existence of situations in conformity with Article 85 and 86.

Smaller undertakings, however, have no choice: if they want the assistance of colleagues there is no other solid solution than a contract or a pseudo-contract in the form of a systematically and rigidly concerted practice. Holdings, concerns and all other kinds of transnational groups, if they want to share the different national markets within the Common Market, do not need such tricks. To put it simply: they publish price-lists, they introduce a distribution and pricing system further and they use the telephone (or 'information systems' of another kind). Of course, they have not only friends but also enemies. Open wars are, however, almost always – although not always smoothly – avoided. Gloves are preferred to weapons. This is of course not a critical remark, it is just a fact.

The consequences of such an attitude based on conscious use of power for the operation of the Common Market are not yet fully appreciated, otherwise jurisprudence in this field would have been as rich as that on exclusivity problems, for example.

B.   Decentralization and co-operation

It is the right of any corporation to decide whether it is profitable or not to operate through separately incorporated subsidiaries. In the first case, the centre of decision of the group may grant the subsidiaries a considerable degree of operational independence. However, this freedom will always be subject to checks. Corporations under central control cannot properly be viewed as really economically independent. Their relationship will inevitably be the result of management decisions rather than of market forces. It is the decision centre of the group which will define the extent of freedom and real independence of the units in the light of profit maximization for the group. Even 'maximizing competition' among the jointly controlled units is in this light a mirage. The criterion is not social welfare but the private welfare of the group. Both may coincide, but this is not always obvious.

This is the normal point of departure for the assessment of the structural and functional characteristics of a transnational group active within the borders of a homogeneous – e.g. the Belgian, German – market. But the question arises whether the EEC Treaty does not require the introduction of specific new political and geographic criteria into the policy under article 85 and 86 of the Treaty concerning transnational groups active in the not yet homogeneous Community.

The transnational corporations consider the whole free world as their market. Optimalization of production is easy in the Common Market in view of the possibilities offered by the already realized free-trade area to fully exploit its possibilities for rationalization. The whole Common Market can be supplied from one optimal production centre instead of from the national centres established in a nationalistic – i.e. less integrated – period. Economies of scale can, in principle, be freely realized and exploited. Nevertheless many observers have pointed out that prices are too often different along both sides of national frontiers. These differences are inexplicable, especially if they are substantial and concern standardized mass products not inherently requiring a sophisticated sales organization or much after-sales servicing. Without conscious market partitioning most price differences are, to say the least, puzzling.

The explanation is that the modern transnational enterprise, active within the Common Market, can maintain geographically differentiated, national prices with the help of territorial exclusivities given by the group to the affiliates established in each country. Italian buyers will in principle not be accepted as clients by French affiliates of an international group. Sales conditions and prices are tailor-made for one specific national or geographic market. A network of branch-establishments and agents make up the rest of the distribution system. The decision centre of the group concentrates on general organization and co-ordination, research, development, finance. Sales activities, especially concerning mass consumption products, are in varying degrees attributed to the national operations. This scheme gives the transnational enterprise the possibility to exploit the differences in the elasticities of the demand in each geographic or national area. Of course, in itself exploitation of different demand curves is not illicit. It becomes, however, suspect if done by enterprises in a dominant position – collective or individual – able to determine more or less effectively the demand and supply curves. And under the EEC Treaty it is all the more suspect if the splits in the price levels follow the historical national borderlines which the Treaty wants to be eliminated.

Of course, operational decentralization within a group is in accordance with modern theory about the organization of the firm. This suggests the delegation of decision making from the higher levels to lower operational units. So it is not astonishing that the degree of spatial and other (de-) centralization within groups is very divergent. A 'holding' – type group guarantees a high degree of autonomy for affiliated firms. Firms active in the sector of mass consumption products are generally of this type. On the other hand, enterprises in the sector of raw materials and basic products are more centralized. The differences are directly connected with the characteristics of the markets in question and buyer preferences.

In these circumstances it is essential to know where in the production and sale of the different products centralization ends and decentralization begins. This knowledge is indispensable for the appreciation of the consequences of the functional decentralization of a group for the unity of the Common 'internal' Market. Normally the management of the production is rather centralized on the basis of product sectors in order to achieve maximal economies of scale. One production unit supplies a number of markets if these markets individually do not offer the possibility for viable production units of optimal size. The unity of the Common Market is then not at stake. However, the danger becomes real at the distribution level when commerical decentralization becomes geographical. Such spatial commerical exclusivities are usually far-reaching. They imply the distribution of the products of the whole group within the borders of any given national market. Price fixing is one of the essential prerogatives of these national operations which may cover hundreds of products.

Evidently this independence within the group – which is not necessarily identical for all national subsidiaries – is seen as the best device for profit maximization. Consequently, and to stress individuality, each national affiliated corporation publishes its own accounts. This characterizes them as real profit centres within the group with all the obligations and honours associated with this position. Often, the opinion of a national affiliate carries great weight. In such a case the centre accepts the role of 'coordinator': it convinces or obliges the other national affiliates to follow the ideas of one of them. This happens frequently in commercial affairs as no affiliate wants to be hindered by an other member of the group. Frequently, the centre of the group plays the role of a market coordinator.

So the structural organization of transnational groups is based on two lines: a vertical one linked with the realization of optimal production for the group, and a horizontal one linked with the distribution on distinct geographical markets. It is the last, the horizontal line which is directly relevant for the unity of the common market. Although exceptional clients may have direct access to the centre of the group, as a rule the production units transfer their products to distribution units with a geographically limited, most purely national, mission. In this structure the national commercial units are the principal clients of the groups' production units and may be considered as the exclusive sellers for the parent company.

C. Intra-enterprise co-operation and Article 85

This screen of dependent independence from the decision centre of the group is continuously changing with the rhythm of costs and profit variations. For a group of firms the use of the play of market forces has its advantages. It often has also its costs and the group centre tries to eliminate these costs. Transaction costs, normal in business between independent producers and clients, are reduced in an aggregated group. Carefully controlled intra-group competition can cut them down and boost the results of the group. So in many cases the decision centre seeks offers for the production of an article from several subsidiaries and accepts only the best one.

The role of the national decision centres of the big transnational groups should be appreciated under Article 85 in the light of this moving structure

67

based on the combined action of dependence and independence. Fundamentally speaking the national centres are specialized cells for which the concept 'Member State' – and not Common Market – is the permanent consideration. Intra-group transfers can always compensate possible disadvantages. So the freedom conceded to national units will be maintained as long as its costs are less than the profits resulting from it. This latitude of action finds its clearest expression in the existence of different price levels between the national markets.

The decision centre may order that all sales by production units to the national subsidiaries have to be effected at uniform ex-works prices. But also then the national directors may prove their independence with different wholesale prices protected as they are behind the walls of their geographical exclusivity. If on the other hand the head office orders differentiated ex-works prices for the products of its factories then it may be suspected of systematic discrimination between geographical, separated, markets. As far as mass-products are concerned a producer will only exceptionally be able to justify these differences with solid socio-economic arguments.

Of course, in case of significant price differences so called parallel imports may occur. This kind of business assumes, however, the presence of independent and aggressive intermediaries. The ways and means by which large corporations force distributors to toe other lines are known: open or hidden vertical integration, substitution of free distributors by agents, special rebate systems or bonifications, rebates on distinct product groups of the diversified corporation, grouping of transport, etc. Inevitably these and other commercial measures of a 'nationalistic' nature have a very negative effect on the unity of the Common Market.

So the national affiliates play a major role in establishing or boycotting the Common Market. To guarantee that this role is only positive Articles 85 and 86 are essential instruments. Situations of abuse under Article 86 will remain as exceptional as clear individual or collective dominant positions. But the national prices surely might be considered under Article 85. Intra-group concertation can be prohibited if some of the conditions indicated in the following questions are fulfilled. Of course, any element has to be weighed. The reader will see that these questions are all related to the degree of operational independence of the affiliated corporations and the extent to which they engage in concerted, joint conduct that concerns third parties:

– Are the structure and size of national subsidiaries and their staff such that they are to be considered operational?
– Do the national companies keep separate records and accounts? Is the intrinsic significance of such account real? In particular, how far are they able, and do they, take risks, and in what ways?
– Do the subsidiaries have a real own responsibility? This responsibility should not be judged only on the basis of legal or purely structural factors.

Crucial is the day-to-day management and the question according to which criteria the managers operate.
- Is the national subsidiary responsible for certain production activities, assembling activities or their organization, for (some) research, transport, sales promotion, etc.?
- Are the subsidiaries' outside sales significant? What are the current relations with other subsidiaries in the other Member States of the Common Market?
- As the activities of the national subsidiaries are, of course, inter-woven, how are the compensations for the commercial, technical, administrative and management services rendered by the subsidiaries amongst each other defined and regulated?
- Does the policy making independence of the national subsidiaries allow them to differ? Do they underline an own national personality? Can factors tending to isolate national subsidiaries be identified?
- How far goes the responsibility concerning profit making of the subsidiaries in question?
- How do national subsidiaries influence the selling prices of the products produced by themselves or 'bought' from other centres of the group? Are there internal transfer prices fixed by the group?
- Which are the arrangements between the group and the national subsidiaries defining the financial relationship between them? What is their character: purely accountable, 'at arms length' or really market oriented?

These questions are only indicative: each situation will invite specific ad hoc questions. But, I think, they are revealing for the definition of the Common Market or 'Internal' market problems to be solved when transnational groups are involved.

The questions show, I hope, that the retrenchment behind the formal verdict that a national subsidiary of a transnational group lives under an all-dominating parent-subsidiary relationship, lacks operational and political depth and reality as far as the EEC Treaty is concerned. The present situation which favours large transnational organizations can only be avoided by appreciating the problem of unity not in the first instance on the level of competition in the legal or classic economic sense of the word but only after the introduction of a specific EEC test of operational unity of the Common 'Internal Market'. When standing on this ground, the central question concerns the discretionary distance between the centre and its affiliates – and among these. If the activities of affiliates prove that its position is that of sub-decision centre it is justified to assume that the group and its affiliates have enough independence to consider co-operation among them as practices aimed at by Article 85 of the Treaty.

It is a fact that the actual working of the (not so!) Common Market proves that many affiliates of transnational groups are considered as active national profit centres. This fact waters down the 'internal' transfer character of commercial transactions between group and affiliates or among affiliates and transforms them in practice into sales. The more affiliates tend to be treated at arms length, the more they should be considered as units sufficiently independent to have discretionary power as to distribution – and to national market sharing – within the Common Market. The legal parent-subsidiary relation does not necessarily exclude the commercial seller-buyer relation if the unity of the Common Market is at stake. This is particularly clear where the centre negotiates directly with exceptional clients and is thus in 'grey' competition with one or more of the national affiliates.

If the national affiliates are not only 'alter egos' of the parent firm and if they are characterized by own sales policies and own prices, they are 'at arms length' from the centre. This transforms intra-enterprise transactions in inter-enterprise transactions with sufficient characteristic features to fall under Article 85, – even if directives replace formal agreements. The 'law of the group' should be considered as inferior to the 'law of European Unity' as instrument for economic integration.

D. The operational approach

The adequate approach to these situations is complex, it is necessary to be inventive. This concerns first the interpretation of the classic market concept. The most usual model of competition is based on action in a relevant market. This worked well in a simple society where the various product markets constituted well defined areas to which more or less classic economic analysis was appropriate. As modern diversified and aggregate corporations are active on many product markets and in many countries, the market concept is not very adequate.

As everybody active in transnational diversified enterprises feels, the market of 'his' firm is unclear. Market analysis cannot predict, define or assess the decisions and attitudes of the directors of multimarket enterprises which are derived from the overall strategy of diversified groups. In order to appreciate and to judge these decisions one has to analyse the group of enterprises itself and not its markets. Competitive action of big corporations is always multidimensional and necessitates a simultaneous analysis of the behaviour on several 'relevant' geographical and product markets. There are many kinds of competition. They have to be appreciated and the separate results have to be integrated in a scheme covering the firm as a complete organizational unit in the light of its – often decisive – influence on the unity of the Common Market.

The existing jurisprudence concerning transnational enterprises with national subsidiaries looks essentially to the form and less to the economic substance. Liability under Article 85 should, however, not depend on whether an enterprise bases its distribution system on agreements with independent distributors, on unincorporated divisions or on wholly owned

70

subsidiaries. The choice, made on legal, economic or other grounds as to the structure of its commercial activities should not be relevant to whether the enterprise's conduct threatens the unity of the Common Market. Common ownership and control should not liberate corporations from the impact of the rules of Article 85. Of course it is not the prime task of corporations to bring about the Common Market. But it cannot be denied that the role of big transnational groups is instrumental to its realization now and in 1992. It is the parents who give their subsidiaries a certain personality of their own. This personality opens the door for often far going market partitioning or sharing. This 'internal allocation of tasks' – as it is chastely called by the enterprises and most lawyers – should be appreciated and depreciated in this light.

As the whole structure of the transnational groups has clear cartellike features, they should pay the price fixed by the EEC Treaty, i.e. submission to the rules defined by Article 85. At present these groups run with the hare by exploiting the unity of the Common Market in creating production units not of national, but of optimal transnational size; but they hunt with the hounds by maintaining commercially divided national pricing systems for the distribution of their products.

This anomaly should find an end – as should a different but equally serious technique of price discrimination which will be dealt with now.

3. Pricing systems

A. Delivered pricing

The situation on the markets for mass products as indicated above in the introduction shows that clear price differences between national markets prove that the traditionally established firms are able to pursue policies without having to reckon with sufficient competition from outside. On the markets of transport-intensive homogeneous mass products and raw materials national market isolation and discrimination is still more explicit and more the rule than the exception. Normally these national price differentiations are the result of concerted practices between oligopolists combined, in the case of transnational groups, with intra-group co-operation. The domain of geographic or spatial pricing has since the beginning of the century been covered by the baptismal name 'basing point pricing'. The on-going use of such pricing practices in all countries has been considered as sufficient evidence of conspiracy. Whether this conspiracy is unlawful is, of course, another question.

Basing point systems are only applied by industries with specific characteristics. Their products are essentially standardized, so that the output of each producer at a given consuming point is a substitute for the output of another producer at that point. This results of course in the same 'equilibrium' prices being charged by the two producers. The products are also low in value per unit weight. So for shipments over longer distances transportation costs form a substantial part of the delivered price. Consequently spatial differentiation of the product price delivered to the consumer can form an essential competitive factor. The optimal scale of operations is large. Capital investment is great per unit of output and – last but not least – the ratio of marginal cost to average cost is low for all rates of operation below optimal capacity. Production equipment is 'heavy' and 'tough'. Closure or restarting of production units is a difficult process. The demand curve is generally inelastic.

An analysis of the American anti-trust jurisprudence shows that the following industries are particularly 'basing point sensitive': iron and steel, coal, oil, cement and other building materials, wood, paper, glass, chemical mass products, basic foodstuffs. The reader will think: 'typical oligopolies!'. This is true, and so these basic problems are strongly interdependent as to output and price. But really voluntary actions by suppliers are necessary to translate the existence of an oligopolistic market into a situation of non-competitive pricing with market sharing.

One of the goals of any producer – oligopolist or not – is a certain market order, requiring specific stabilizing instruments. 'Basing point pricing' is the 'crux'. Its outstanding feature is the creation of a well-defined and well-published price structure with clear delivered (c.i.f.) prices. The delivered prices of suppliers are then identical for all consumers at each specific location or in each specific region. The effective operation of this system requires 'basing points' and 'base prices', i.e. prices calculated and invoiced by several single producers as if the products were shipped at one given factory, station or port although the distance between the different production units is often considerable. Uniformly defined freight costs from every basing point to every consuming point complete this picture.

Such 'basing points' have long been critically regarded as contrary to public welfare and discriminatory in the economic sense of the word. In point of fact, buyers who are located nearer to the plant, from which the shipments are actually made, than to the basing point indicated by the seller, are required to pay non-existent freight charges. These charges constitute price discrimination between the nearby buyers who have to pay the burden of a non-existent freight for their competitors who are situated at greated distance of the basing point who pay too little freight costs.

Prof. L. Phlips, who made a study for the European Commission on 'Spatial Pricing and Competition' (1976) indicated in a later elaboration 'The Economics of Price Discrimination' (1983) that 'discrimination might be as common in the market place as it is rare in economic textbooks'. It is true that not all forms of discrimination are a direct dangers for the unity of the 'internal' market. But it is striking that in the jurisprudence of the Community even the clear dangers of this commerical geographical – or spatial – phenomenon are largely absent. This is astonishing. Geographical or spatial prices, as too numerous sellers and buyers know, are extremely frequent. They may be applied by national or transnational manufacturing groups or by the predominant manufacturer in the industry, acting as the 'price-leader'[3]. It is usual in most modern industries to consider concertedly a colleague competitor as regional leader. They may also result from a more simple interaction of independent pricing policies of the individual manufacturers located at or near the particular basing point.

The different types of basing point pricing do not have the same impact on the correct or incorrect working of the Common Market. The most dangerous type is that of identical delivered prices on the part of a dominant manufacturer or group of manufacturers at any destination in a specific country or other large geographic area, regardless of the variations in transportation costs. In order to be effective this actual identity of delivered prices at all destination points, based on dominance or resulting from the concerted observance of a particular pricing system, requires participants to engage in various ancillary activities or implementing measures. Such ancillary measures may include for example the refusal to sell on an ex-works or f.o.b. basis, common freight rate books to ensure uniform use of the same common trasnportation cost factors, uniform price 'extra's', common action against foreign imports, etc. If the trade is disciplined enough and strict control of destination is possible, the producer may allow reimbursement of freight costs when delivery is taken at the factory.

A zone pricing system, so dangerous for the unity of the Common Market, is feasible only if a market lends itself for being split up geographically by market-sharing agreements or concerted practices. This is, in the European context, rather easy if the definition of the different markets to be shared follows the national borderlines. If applied in this way there can be no competition at the production or wholesale level. Above all, buyers are cornered and have in principle no incentive to obtain supplies from sources nearer by. So the spatial configuration of delivered prices may maximize the profits of the dominant firm or the joint profits of the (relatively small) group of firms applying it. These systems have as decisive advantage that, once put into operation, they are self-perpetuating in the sense that renewed understandings are not needed to maintain identical delivered prices over an indefinite period time.

B.   Article 85 and geographical pricing

It is necessary to translate this general consideration into an operational terminology adapted to the necessities of the EEC-Treaty concerning market unity. It is evident that no firm active within the Common Market will be so reckless as to publish for its products a price ex-works of 100 for German, 110 for French and 120 for Italian buyers. If it wants to exploit differences in the demand curve of the separate Member States – no matter

73

whether these differences are 'natural' or artifically created and maintained by the firms themselves – it masks its intentions by only quoting 'delivered' prices, that is, by not only supplying the product but also taking care of transport. The principal goal is, as we saw, to make sure that, at a given place, identical prices are quoted by the different sellers. This is the 'trademark' of the system whose principal feature is that a seller making use of uniform delivered prices can easily separate geographical markets. So, competition on the basis of distance – i.e. transport – is diminished or completely eliminated. It is possible here to use an identical pattern of zone delivered pricing per Member State or a uniform price system in a specific zone. If firms in a concentrated industry wish to avoid disturbances and if they are not allowed to establish common sales agencies or other forms of close commercial co-operation, a satisfactory expedient is provided by basing point systems and delivered zone pricing.

Such a formula-based delivered price system – like all others – is clearly restrictive of competition as it supposes a restraint upon a seller's selfinterest to enlarge his market share in certain local markets by means of unsystematic price reductions. It is evident that no seller's selfinterest would permit him to continue to engage in such pricing unless he is sure most rivals will continue to engage in the common practice of delivered pricing, at the same level. Uncertainties, unleashed by independent variations in ex-works process, are avoided.

Contemporary end of the 20th century delivered price systems can be relatively easily established and perpetuated in the Common Market without formal assistance of explicitly co-operative cartel-like procedures. Informal concertation is largely sufficient. Evidence of an economic nature to prove practices contrary to Article 85 and 86 of the EEC Treaty can, however, easily be found: the basis is an inventory of the prices applied on the different regional or national markets and an appreciation of the systems behind them. And here I cannot resist the temptation to cite a review of the well-known political economist J.K. Galbraith, published in Fortune (April 1949), of the classic book by Machlup: The Basing-Point System. Machlup was a successful businessman before he became a renowned economist. He knew the working of the market. These lines suggest some limits of the power of the legal discipline when the realization of a real union in the Common Market is at stake.

'The basing-point system of pricing is the most intricately confusing phenomenon of modern capitalism. Professor Machlup attributes most of the thirty-year uncertainty about its legality to the inability of judges to understand it. One difficulty is that its outward mechanics is benignly simple, whereas there is nothing simple whatsoever about its consequences'.

It is zone-delivered pricing systems, which are at the core of many signs of disunion within our Common Market. If the approach of the Articles 85 and

86 of the EEC Treaty really is that of a united 'internal' market, it is clear that persistent, industry-wide price discrimination within this common geographic market should certainly alert to a real and substantial possibility of collusion. Within a homogeneous economy – the American, British, French, etc. – zone pricing may not be as simple to achieve, because functionally the method of drawing zone boundaries is not inherently responsive but generally contains an element of arbitrariness. Unfortunately this responsiveness is until now omnipresent within the boundaries of the Common Market because of the deeply rooted nationalistic instincts. Therefore it looses in the public commercial eye its arbitrariness. But this does not mean that the arguments in favour of spatial, geographic pricing within the Common Market as presented by the transnational corporations should be accepted without extremely critical consideration. In fact, national pricing systems pose the problem of price discrimination in a geographic, i.e. European market which pretends to be a unity. It is less and less justified to tacitly accept clear price frontiers between the Member States with significant price differences between them based on spatially and nationally circumscribed pricing systems.

Naturally a firm should move away from narrow profit margins to the wider ones, from less profitable to more profitable markets. This happens in the national markets, and should occur *a fortiori* also in the growing Common Market with an evolving rice structure. Fixed different national price structures present therefore a problem to even the least critical Common Market observer. These differentiations – which are clear discriminations in the legal sense – have a tremendous negative effect on the free movement of goods between the Member States. The systems in question should be considered as falling in the category of *per se* prohibitions not only as they increase the ability of powerful firms to detect non-conformance to the shared monopoly consensus but, more specifically in the EEC-context, as this consensus has clear anti-Common Market purposes and results.

4. Conclusion

My conclusion – and conviction! – is clear: suppression of legal barriers complicating trade on a real Common Market scale will not automatically result in non-nationalistic prices as long as important transnational manufacturers have the possibility not only to push the distributors under a strong discipline but, more importantly: to organize without danger for critical remarks their own price systems on a national basis. I suggested already that often the head office of a group is less interested in protection of national markets than its national subsidiaries. Consequently the manufacturer often represents the interests of his distributors in something which is, in practice, a sales cartel: against price competition, against violation of territorial rights. So, the manufacturer of the decision centre of the group degenerates more or less into an agent of its national affiliates in the administration of a market sharing cartel. Viewed from the level of the objectives of the Treaty I do not think that this presentation is exaggerated. So the price systems applied by the big groups active in Europe strongly contribute to the consolidation of the existing national structures. The first clear transnational pricing systems still seem to have to be born – except for the ECSC industries. Is it not necessary for all public and private parties to stimulate such a birth before 1992?

Of course: a Single 'Internal' Market should have been completed many years ago. Especially the great transnational corporations regret its absence. But they should not only point the finger of scour to the national administrations but also dive into their own bossom. The role that these corporations can play to stimulate the Single European Market has since the entry into force of the EEC Treaty been underestimated for thirty years. They do not need an official step of a legal nature to start on their own initiative the introduction of pro-community pricing formulas or systèmes de prix communautaires. From my own experience I know the complexity of such a task. But it is undoubtedly an essential part of the 1992 objective.

In the meantime the transnational groups should adapt the weight and the number of stones they cast to the European Institutions to the progress they make with the introduction of 'community pricing...'

VI.   Joint ventures under the competition rules of the EEC-Treaty

B. VAN DER ESCH[1]

1.   Introduction

The context of this publication suggests the following plan:

– general description of the nature of the problem and of the main legal and administrative parameters;
– limits of the applicability of Article 85(1) to joint ventures;
– exemptions;
– some recent cases.

This contribution does not propose to trace the whole history of the subject, nor to analyse all the cases and deal with all their ramifications. It has the more limited objective of describing more recent developments, mostly from the Thirteenth Report on Competition Policy onwards. That report, which covers the activities of 1983, restates very clearly the Commission's view on the applicability of Article 85(1) to joint ventures and contains a first effort to define realistic parameters for this applicability.[2]

2.   The nature of the problem

Joint ventures are a major instrument of assignment and redeployment of production factors, of optimal use of resources, of constant adjustment of the latter to changing circumstances.

Mobility of capital and labour are of the essence of industrial vigour and health. An application of the Competition rules which would cripple these dynamics would be incompatible with Article 2 of the Treaty, would disregard the obligations of Article 87(2) c and d and would be generally

---

[1] Formerly Senior Legal Counsellor for Competition to the Commission of the European Communities; special Counsel to De Brauw en Westbroek, advocaten en notarissen, 's-Gravenhage.
All opinions expressed are in the author's personal capacity. Thanks are due to Helmuth Schröter who read the manuscript and made valuable suggestions.
[2] *Commission Thirteenth Report on competition policy (1984)* p. 50 *ff.*

counterproductive to everything the Community stands for, politically as well as economically. The competitive strength of community industries in increasingly global markets is vital for the achievement of all community goals.

The emphasis placed by the competition rules of the Treaty on the merits of the individual effort of the market participants, free of collusion with others, does not imply a blanket condemnation of all co-operation between firms. Certain types and/or circumstances of co-operation are not apprehended by Article 85(1), others are exempted or exemptible. It is the diversity and multiplicity of industrial and commercial arrangements reached in the framework of joint ventures which have made it difficult to define precisely these categories and the borderlines which separate them. Nevertheless, gradually a pattern has been emerging, first from policy statements and individual decisions and then, more recently, from the work on guidelines for the assessment of co-operative joint ventures under Article 85 EEC.

The approach is two-pronged:

– co-operative deployment or redeployment of production factors, is welcomed in principle
but
– whenever perceptible restrictions of competition are agreed or engendered, wherever perceptible distortions of competition are created, public control operates under the conditions of Article 85(1) sanctioned by the nullity of Article 85(2) and combined, where appropriate, with the decision-making power of the Commission. This two-pronged approach is in conformity with Article 85(1) which prohibits certain anti-competitive effects of entrepreneurial behaviour. The organization or emergence of anti-competitive market structures is one of these effects. Whatever the virtues of many co-operative joint ventures, the instrument as such should not become a means of side-stepping Article 85.[3]

In their simplest expression – two parent companies and one joint venture – joint ventures are triangles of co-operation in the market assigned to them. Regularly, overlap or interference occurs between that field of activity and the autonomous operations of the parents in the same or related markets.

Joint ventures are widely used. Every year numerous triangles, quadrangles or even larger constellations are formed.[4] For the reasons indicated

[3] *Commission 16th Report on competition policy (1987)* p. 43.
[4] *16th Report on Competition Policy (1987)* p. 232 where the formation of joint ventures is examined in the context of concentration and rationalisation of industry and services. Between the 1,000 biggest firms of the Community, in the period 1982–1986, 278 joint ventures were formed, apart from 284 minority participations and 706 majority participations or mergers. Within a larger sample of nearly 2,300 financial operations not limited to the 1,000 biggest firms 368 industrial joint ventures were counted (*ibidem* p. 244). The report is silent, unfortunately, on the number of notifications of joint ventures.

78

above, Article 85 applies to the effects on competition as to the effects outside it on the structure of the relevant market. While leaving ample scope for co-operation which creates new competition, Article 85 also requires that a legitimate combination of efforts does not degenerate into a permanent non-competition clause, pact or practice in a significant part of the market. By means of a joint venture firms may shape their *presence* in the market in a more competitive manner and quite often Article 85(1) will not even apply. However, the application of Article 85(1) begins with certainty where co-operation between significant market participants *modifies the market structure* or where such participants regulate their own and the joint-ventures' *behaviour* in the market.

An example in point is furnished by the Wano/Schwarz-pulver decision.[5] A deployment within a joint venture of production factors which was rational in itself was vitiated because the parent companies also wished to partition the Common Market. Such clauses or practices are inevitably caught by Article 85(1) and will normally not be *exemptible*, in accordance with established administrative practice and case law.

Frequently, the creation of an improved presence in the market, of a better basis for participation in the competitive process, is accompanied by restrictive clauses within the triangle designed to ensure a reasonable industrial or commercial viability of the joint venture, in relation to its parents. If limited in time and scope, such clauses may be considered inherent in the creation of the joint venture and ancillary to its proper functioning. As the principal commands the secondary, such restrictions do not justify by themselves an application of Article 85(1) to the joint venture in question.

Restrictive clauses over and above the threshold of ancillarity bring Article 85(1) into play, even for joint ventures which create new competition. In these cases exemption is necessary. The criteria of Article 85(3) will have to be fulfilled, once more in conformity with established administrative practice and case law. No exemption is available to joint ventures which distort competition in a substantial part or segment of the Common Market to the point of eliminating its normal effects.

This broad description of the main thrust of competition policy in the field of joint ventures still leaves an unnecessary degree of legal insecurity for industry and its advisors. To a certain extent market participants can remedy this themselves by reducing the restrictive clauses on parents and on the joint venture alike, in other words by allowing for more risks within the triangle or constellation. However, this self-control is no substitute for an adequate administrative control of joint ventures as required by Article 87(2) EEC. The responsibility for this control continues to rest with the Commission. It has the duty to uphold workable competition while leaving adequate scope for co-operative deployment of production factors. A proper

---

[5] OJ 1978 L 322 p. 26 *ff. Commission 8th Report on competition policy (1979) p. 98 ff.*

balance between these two objectives can only be struck by an application of Article 85(1) which is both selective and flexible. Sufficient scope for such a balance exists, as will be demonstrated below.

Before proceeding with that demonstration, one technique of simplification of the problem should be discussed separately and rejected.

Some authors continue to plead that all joint ventures set up for a lasting role in the market and provided with the necessary corporate means and functions to that effect, should be considered as merger-like operations between the parents which remain outside Article 85 for the reasons set out in the 1965 Commission Memorandum 'The Problem of Mergers in the Common Market'.[6] According to these writers the dominant features of a joint venture are the financial participations, and the ensuing changes on the corporate level, which the authors of the Treaty have not wanted to put under a community system of merger control. Ergo Article 85(1) does not apply to the creation of that type of joint venture, unles it is accompanied by explicitly restrictive clauses between the parents or unless complementary concerted practices can be discerned.

This reasoning was never convincing and is less and less so. At present it is more doubtful than ever that the absence of rules for merger control in the EEC Treaty should carry greater weight for the interpretation of the competition rules than the constitutional principle of Article 3f according to which undistorted competition must be maintained. In other words, it is less and less certain that the non-application of Article 85 to all true merger operations is still wholly in conformity with the intentions of the authors of the Treaty, as expressed in Article 3f thereof.[6a]

Be this how it may, with a few exceptions, to which we will return later, joint ventures fall far short of mergers and there is therefore even less reason to claim immunity from scrutiny under Article 85 just because a capital participation is involved. The tail of capital participation cannot wag the dog of the competition rules. On the contrary, as there are no indications in the Treaty that capital participations automatically fall outside Article 85, the legal certainty of the preservation of a system of undistorted competition requires that wherever such participations do carry a risk of distortion of competition, the prohibition of Article 85(1) applies, unless an exemption under Article 85(3) has been given.

The question whether Article 85(1) applies to the acquisition by a com-

---

[6] *See* Holger, Wissel, 'Gemeinschaftsunternehmen im EWG Kartell-recht. Eine Erwiderung, *FIW Schriftenreihe* Heft 122, Köln 1987. *Aeso* C. Iliopolous, Gemeinschaftsunternehmen im EGKS- und EWG-Kartellrecht, Baden-Baden 1986, reviewed by the present author in Cahiers de Droit Europeen, 1987, p. 379.

[6a] After these words were written, the Commission applied Article 85 in an informal procedure to a merger between two manufacturers of tin cans, because of a substantial minority participation of a third competitor in the capital of the merged unit, Commission's Press Release January 1988.

pany of a substantial equity interest in a competitor arose in some recent Commission decisions. The Commission considered that Article 85(1) could be applied in principle, but it rejected the complaints lodged by certain cigarette manufacturers against such an acquisition. These decisions have been confirmed by the Court of Justice.[7]

Effective applicability of Article 85(1) arises where either by a shareholding or through subsidiary clauses, legal or de facto control over the commercial conduct of another company is obtained.[8]

This ruling implies that where two or more competitors create or obtain such control over another company the same reasoning may be validly applied. The applicability of Article 85(1) to substantial equity participations in a competitor developes into the finding of an infringement, where it can be shown that the agreements are the basis of an investment – even a passive one – have the object or effect of influencing the competitive behaviour of the companies concerned on the relevant market.[9] The same burden of proof has to be acquitted before it may be validly found that a joint venture comes within the interdiction of Article 85(1).

The support provided by the BAT judgment for the application of Article 85(1) to joint ventures is not reduced by the fact that the case in point concerned a stagnant and oligopolistic market. Circumstances of that kind are important for the evidence required, especially in cases of substantial minority participations, but they do not limit the applicability of Article 85(1) as such.

In view of the above it may be concluded that as of the date of the judgment in question the legal basis for the application of Article 85(1) to a considerable number of joint ventures is properly secured. It is on this basis, that we now turn to the scope of Article 85(1) and (3), as it results from the Commission's administrative practice and relevant case law.

3.   Limits on the applicability of Article 85(1)

Many types of co-operation between firms are devoid of anti-competitive effect and are therefore not prohibited by Article 85(1). These types are enumerated in the Notice on Co-operation between enterprises.[10] The use of a joint venture does not affect this assessment. Joint ventures, the parents and the object of which remain within the limits of that Notice

---

[7] Cases 142 and 155/84, *BAT and Reynolds vs Commission,* 17 November 1987, not yet reported (more particularly Ground 37). Previously, Advocated-General Mancini also agreed with the Commission's thesis that a substantial holding in a competitor is likely to distort competition. (Opinion of 17 March 1987 p. 29).

[8] *Ibidem*, Ground 38.

[9] *Ibidem*, Ground 45.

[10] OJ 1968 C 75, p. 3.

benefit from the presumption expressed therein that Article 85(1) does not apply.

A similar presumption operates for joint ventures which remain within the Notice on Agreements of minor importance, as modified by a decision of the Commission of 3 September 1986.[11] The quantitive limits set therein on the application of Article 85(1) are a far from negligeable 5% market share and combined maximum turnover of participants of 200 million ECU. Unofficially it has been suggested to adopt for joint ventures as a more structed form of co-operation a higher threshold of perceptibility. A 15% market share has been mentioned.[12] Below that limit structural anti-competitive effects are indeed not very likely. In order not to stretch the underlying concept of perceptibility, it would be prudent to require in addition that restrictions on the market behaviour of a joint venture or of its partners should remain limited to what is strictly necessary for the initial viability of the joint venture in relation to the partners and that they should lapse after 5 years. Only the restrictions that prevent the partners from threatening this viability may be considered as truly ancillary and benefit from the main presumption of inapplicability of Article 85(1).[13]

The two preceeding limits on the applicability of Article 85(1) are well established rules. Their interpretation is moreover relatively easy. A more complex but nevertheless realistic limit arises where co-operation between firms is an objective *conditio sine qua non* for an extension of their activity in a new market or for their continued participation in an existing market on a more competitive industrial basis. In these cases, entry by only one of the venturers – or unilateral improvement of the competitive basis – is not a realistic alternative to the joint venture. The creation of this joint venture is therefore not restrictive of competition as such. It may become so as a result of additional restrictive clauses or of substantial foreclosure of the market.

In order to avoid misunderstanding, the fact of requiring evidence of a real restriction of competition between the joint ventures, before applying Article 85(1) should not be confused with the balancing of the anti-competitive and pro-competitive effects of the joint-venture. Such balancing would undoubtedly be preferred by some advocates of the introduction of a rule of reason in Community competition law.[14] The focus of the real-

[11] OJ 1986 C 231, p. 2.
[12] Speech of Mr. Sutherland of 7 November 1985 IP 85 (498).
[13] On the ancillary restrictions doctrine see M. Waelbroeck in 1987 Fordham Corporate Law Institute, B. Hawk Ed.
[14] V. Korah, 'EEC Competition Policy, Legal Form or Economic Efficiency,' 1986 *Current Legal Problems* p. 85; M.C. Schechter, The Rule of Reason in European Competition Law, 1882 Legal Issues of European Integration, Part 2, p. 1 *ff.*; I. Forrester and C. Norall, The Laicization of Community Law Self Help and The Rule of Reason, *21 Common Market Law Review*, p. On this subject *also see:* P. Ulmer, Rule of Reason im Rahmen von Artikel 85 EWGV, *Recht der Internationalen Wirtschaft* 1985 p. 517 *ff.* R. Kovar, 'Le droit communautaire de la concurrence et la règle de la raison', *Revue Trimestrielle de droit européen*, 1987, p. 237 ss.

82

restriction test is much narrower and more precise. The burden of proof contains the demonstration that an individual effort is not a viable alternative for the firms concerned. This goes well beyond the subjective preference that may be expressed by the firms involved. The assessment of the competitive relationship between the partners should be objective. A useful instrument for such an objective assessment is the checklist for the evaluation of the degree of potential competition between the partners contained in the Thirteenth Report on Competition already referred to (see paragraph 1). Only if the parents are clearly competitors on the level of single action, the application of Article 85(1) appears to be justified.

The beneficiaries of this limit are likely to be medium enterprises which exceed the thresholds of the Notice on Agreements of minor importance but whose combined efforts do not make them into major market participants. As in the case of a higher threshold of quantitive perceptibility (see above), only truly ancillary restrictions can be agreed. Restrictive clauses in the agreement which go beyond the creation of normal conditions of industrial and/or commercial viability of the joint venture in relation to the partners would bring the matter back within Article 85(1). As to the potential anti-competitive effects on future competition between the venturers in related markets, these also may bring the creation of the joint venture back within Article 85(1) EEC. Between small and medium enterprises this would, however, appear to be an unlikely hypothesis.

On this point a semantic choice has to be made. Restrictions which protect the viability of the joint venture against possible threats from the partners are truly ancillary and share the fate of the joint venture.

The effects of these restrictions could be called imperceptible, because they result necessarily from any co-operation in the form of a joint venture. This semantic choice would widen the notion of imperceptibility to the quality, the nature, of the restrictions involved. In this sense the concept of minor importance has both a qualitative and a quantitative aspect.

A last substantive limit on the applicability of Article 85(1) applies to joint ventures that qualify as a partial or quasi-concentration. Economic realism not only compels recognition of the special features of market entry joint ventures between medium sized enterprises, but it also requires the recognition of market exit situations.

The Commission has done so in its SHV Chevron decision.[15] As an early attempt in the matter, the decision is not free from weaknesses. The Commission recognises in these decisions that a simultaneous decision by two competing firms to withdraw definitely from a given market, to give up production and sale in that market and to combine all the resources they had to that effect in a joint venture, which is free to dispose of these

---

[15] *Commission 4th Report on Competition policy (1975)* p. 81. The approach followed in this decision has not always been judged correctly. *See* e.g. B. Hawk, *US Common Market and International anti-trust*, Vol. II, p. 260.

resources, is not restrictive of competition within the meaning of Article 85(1). Whether one calls this a partial concentration or not is really irrelevant. It is the facts of life that count and not the name or the label.

It is true that the correct perception of this phenomenon is sometimes blurred by the fact that also in this case the firms involved include restrictive clauses of an ancillary nature. The concentrative nature of the operation remains, however, dominant, provided the clauses in question do no more than to protect the irreversibility of the operation.

4. Exemptions of joint ventures under Article 85(3)

Block exemptions are in force in respect of co-operation in the field of specialisation and of research and development.[16]

Within their field of application these exemptions cover co-operation in the form of a joint venture (see contribution by Lauwaars).

Other block exemptions exist or are envisaged for transfer of technology in the form of patent licences[17] or know-how licences.[18] They offer limited possibilities for parties not only to organise intelligently their presence in the market but also to control their respective behaviour in the market. Licensees can be territorially protected against both active and passive competition from the licensor and other licensees.

Where such clauses appear in a licensing agreement linked to a joint venture, Article 5.1(2) of Regulation 2349/84, excludes them from the benefit of the block-exemption if the joint venture is between competitors. It does not preclude the possibility of an individual exemption. Article 5.1(3) and Article 5.2 moderate this exclusion for certain limited constructions which may include joint ventures, provided no territorial protection is granted. On balance, however, this block-exemption covers only territorial restriction in patent licensing agreements concerning joint ventures between non-competitors.

Apart from these block-exemptions, individual exemptions can be given for joint ventures between parents capable of individual entry into the domain envisaged for the joint venture and which are therefore in potential competition for such entry. If the Notices referred to above do not apply, the restrictive effects of the joint control and/or of the specific restrictive clauses or practices, are caught by Article 85(1). Where that is the case, the limits of exemptibility of Article 85(3) must be respected.[20] A recent and

---

[16] Commission Regulation 417/85 of 19 December 1984, OJ 1985 L53/1.
Commission Regulation 418/85 of 19 December 1984, OJ 1985 L53/5.
[17] Commission Regulation 2349/84 of 23 July 1984, OJ 1984 L219/15.
[18] Draft regulation for a block-exemption for know-how licenses OJ 1987 C 214 p. 2 *ff.*
[19] Article 1(1) 1–6.
[20] Cf. the specialisation agreement between Volvo Flyg Motor and Saner Getriebe which fell outside group exemption 417/85 and was informally declared compatible with Article 85(3) (*15th Report* p.78).

84

complete summary of these limits can be found in the newest addition to the major works on community Law, Lord Hailsham Ed. Halsbury's Law of the European Communities (London, 1986 para. 19–396) to which the reader is referred. One additional remark only is called for. It is of great importance that in case of dissolution of the joint venture full and normal competition re-emerges promptly between the parents. Absence of provisions to that effect cast a shadow on the exemptibility.[21]

5. Some recent individual decisions and notices issued by virtue of Article 19(3) Regulation 17

Recent Commission practice provides examples of non-restrictive co-operation, R and D co-operation, joint ventures for market entry situations and for rationalisation efforts of various depths and intensities, including market exit of the parents. Brief reference is made to each of these cases. The comments are based on published information which does not always give a precise insight in the reasoning of the Commission. Improvement in this respect is clearly possible and desirable.

Three reprocessors of nuclear fuels, whose previous joint venture benefited from an exemption under Article 85(3),[22] modified the terms of their co-operation. The co-ordination of investment and the joint marketing were abandoned and the co-operation reduced to exchange of information in respect of research and development and in respect of the furtherance of more[23] general interests of the parties. It can only be surmised whether these interests center on and are limited to the defence of the reprocessing idea as such, as opposed to storage of spent nuclear fuels. The precise status of the R and D co-operation is not clear. The language of the 16th Report suggests specialisation and exchange of results, but no reference is made to the block-exemptions in these areas. At any rate what sounds like an informal negative clearance is the result. Naturally, if the co-operation in matters of general interest included activities such as sharing of markets, these activities would be null and void and subject to fines.

A recent Notice under Article 19(3) of Regulation 17 concerns R and D co-operation in a joint venture between two manufacturers of packing material and filling machines.[24] The object of the co-operation is the development of a new type of packing for foodstuffs with solid parts such as soups, sauces, vegetables etc.. This packing would consist of lined paperplate (cardboard) with a removable lid, capable of being filled and sealed asepti-

---

[21] Cf. already to that effect the De Laval-Stork decision OJ 1977 L 215, p. II *ff*, *Commission seventh Report on competition policy (1978)*, p. 115.
[22] *Commission 5th Report on competition policy (1976)* p. 42 *ff*.
[23] *Commission 16th Report on competition policy (1987)* p. 85.
[24] *Elopak/Metalbox – ODIN*, OJ 1987 C 215 p. 3 *ff*.

cally. The research includes the development of related filling and treatment machines.

The mass-packing market is oligopolistic. Both partners are highly qualified in their respective fields. The pooling of resources – mostly non-exclusive patent and know-how licenses – is, however, more promising than individual product development. The research-work will be done by the respective parents on contract basis at the request of the joint venture. The new product may compete, at least partially, with existing products of both parents, but mostly with those of Metal Box.

The Notice states that Regulation No. 418/85 does not apply without explaining why. Probably the parties intended to sell the jointly developed and manufactured product through their joint venture to potential product uses. According to Article 2 of Regulation 418/85 joint sales do not benefit from the block-exemption.

The Commission announced its intention of taking a positive decision whether this decision is an exemption or a negative clearance remains unclear. Logically it would have to be an exemption, as the agreement provides for joint exploitation of results without time limit.

Market entry situations underlie the optical fibre joint ventures between Corning/Glass and its two European partners, BICC and Siemens, and the joint venture between Mitchell Cotts and Sofiltra.

In the first case[25] Article 85(1) was applicable to the joint ventures in question only because of their interrelationship and their insertion in a network of other agreements. The initial text of the agreements provided Corning with undisputable leverage for collusion and market-sharing.

After objections from the Commission significant changes were made.[26] As a result Corning Technology obtained market access through the joint ventures but day to day management and sales policies were individually determined by each joint venture without being territorially restricted.

The Mitchell Cotts/Sofiltra case[27] concerned high technology air filters. Sofiltra as the technologically more advanced parent co-operates with the main British user of its product for the purpose of manufacturing in Great Britain. Sofiltra extends its manufacturing base into the UK, strengthened by a stable outlet. Mitchell Cotts integrates upwards into the manufacturing of the main component of its own product for which it lacked both the know-how and the R and D capability of autonomous entry.

The applicability of Article 85(1) resulted mainly from an exclusive licence granted by Sofiltra to the joint venture and from the territorial restrictions agreed upon within the triangle. Even if the agreement had been a straight-forward licence arrangement, without a joint venture, these restrictions

---

[25] *Commission 16th Report on competition policy (1987)* p. 81. OJ 1986 L 236 p. 30.
[26] IP (86) 369.
[27] *Commission 16th Report on competition policy (1987)* p. 83. OJ 1987 L 41 p. 31.

would not have been covered by Regulation 2349/84. Furthermore they are not limited in time. In the course of the assessment under Article 85(1) the decision states that because of the absence of such a time limit, the restrictions were not indispensable. What is probably meant is that, had there been a time limit, certain restrictions could have been considered ancillary and could have remained outside Article 85(1). Although the application of Article 85(1) seems correct the language of the decision is muddled. The decision does not become clearer by the approach of a number of other restrictions. Some of these are inherent in the transfer of know-how. Others could have been declared ancillary (in the sense of the word proposed above) and could therefore have remained outside Article 85(1). The assessment of these restrictions bypassed, however, these substantive questions and limited itself to the finding that they had no appreciable restrictive effect in the context in which they occurred. Again, the result appears defensible but the reasoning is clumsy, to say the least.

Restructuring the petro-chemical industry of the Community has given rise to the creation of a number of joint ventures each designed to give a better chance to the more efficient units of the parent companies and to close down their less modern installations. This approach of the industry reflects the Commission's policy not to allow the formation of all embracing crisis-cartels within oligopolies of this kind.

Two formal decisions have been given so far.

First, BP Chemicals and ICI[28] sold to each other their most modern PVC (polyvinylchloride) and LDPE (low density polyethylene) units. They also sold the goodwill for the products concerned, including the goodwill for quantities produced by older units which were not transferred. In addition certain supply agreements were concluded.

The respective ranges of industrial activity were thus reduced and each firm could improve its performance within the activity on which it concentrated. Unprofitable installations could be closed unilaterally with less disruption for downstream activities. The agreements, considered in their totality, amounted to an agreed reduction of available supplies and, because of the transfer of all goodwill, contained an implicit non-competition clause. Article 85(1) clearly applied. The parties tried to present the result as a partial concentration and to obtain a negative clearance. However, too many distinctive features pointed in the other direction and the argument was rejected. An exemption was granted for the remaining 14 years duration of the agreements. It was based on the prospect of a healthier industrial

---

[28] Decision of 19 July 1984, OJ 1984 L 212 p. 1 *ff; Commission 14th Report on competition policy (1985)* p. 71. N.B. *ibidem* the joint venture partnership between Shell and Akzo (Rovin).

structure embedded in sufficiently effective competition to protect consumer interests.

More recently another exemption was granted for a comparable restructuring plan between Ente Nazionale Idrocarburi and Montedison.[29] Different products were involved, including cracking products which are produced in fixed combinations. Specialisation within the mix of derivatives creates the need for rational outlets of remaining products. Supply and management contracts completed the reciprocal transfer of installations.

As both parties continue to dispose of cracking capacity, potential competition for the activities transferred remained unaffected. This potential competition was, however, neutralised by an express non-competition clause for the first five years and by an implied non-competition clause thereafter. No claim of partial concentration was made. An exemption was granted on the same grounds and for the same duration as in the BP/ICI case.

Yet another co-operative rationalisation joint venture in petro-chemicals is described in a recent notice under Article 19(3) of Regulation 17, Enichem/ICI.[30] The rationalisation concerns the VCM (vinylchloridemonomer) and PVC (polyvinylchloride) activities of the parents. In essence the joint venture, called European Vinyls Corporation, is a common co-ordination center, which implements rationalisation measures concerning R and D and production activities. The joint venture agreement also foresees a closure-programme of certain installations. Classical cartel features largely dominate the legal framework chosen. EVC that is to say the joint management, also controls the sales of the jointly managed production units. The supply of raw materials to EVC by the parents is more or less divided equally between the parents at prices which are fixed by a raw materials committee – composed of the parents and the joint venture. So the rationalisation-cartel contains a price-cartel as well. Technology is pooled but without titles being transferred. The same applies to production capacity. The parents agree not to compete with the joint venture. Plastifiers, used in PVC production, are the subject of an additional agreement. EVC acts as a common sales agent for both parents in the greater part of the Community on the basis of what looks like an implicit market sharing agreement.

In view of the structural overcapacity of the sector, the whole arrangement makes industrial sense. Rather than scrapping outright and unilaterally superfluous installations, the cost of disinvestment is tempered by the intelligent use of complementarities between the two firms.

The notice envisages an exemption for 5 years on condition that the co-operation between the parties does not extend to other firms. At the

---

[29] Decision of 4 December 1986, OJ 1987 L 5 p. 13 *ff. Commission 16th Report on competition policy (1987)* p. 76.
[30] OJ 1987 C 217, p. 2 *ff.* After these words were written the Commission took an official decision, OJ 1988, L 50 p. 18.

expiry of the exemption full and normal competition will have to take the place of the present co-operation.

A last example concerns a set of agreements between Montedison of Italy and Hercules of the US in the domain of polypropylene. In their initial form these agreements amounted to restrictive co-ordination of markets behaviour between two competitors within a joint venture called Himont.[31] As no rationalisation measures were envisaged, overlap between the markets of the parents and of Himont remained a permanent reason for continued co-ordination. So, exemption was not possible.

As a result, the parties modified the agreements. Himont was made into a separate viable entity with real independence from the parents. This independence was achieved by issuing 20% of Himont's Common Stock to the public. Furthermore, the parents abandoned all direct activitives within the EEC in the downstream market of Himont. To that extent a market exit or concentrative feature appeared which, although not as clear as in the SHV/ Chevron case, became nevertheless very significant. This feature was strengthened by the fact that Himont took over the marketing of its own products in the major Member States. The initial supply purchasing agreements within the triangle were also abandoned. Himont will deal with its parents at arm's length.

To quote the Press notice:

> 'In fact Montedison and Hercules have withdrawn completely and permanently as independent operators from the new company's sphere of activity: they no longer operate in related sectors – including upstream and downstream markets – except for activities of minor economic importance in relation to Himont's operation. Furthermore Himont is constituted as a permanent business enterprise and is an independent economic entity capable of taking decisions in its own and its public shareholders' interests.'

Because of these various characteristics the joint venture took on the nature of a permanent redeployment of production factors on a more viable basis. The concentration aspects of the agreement between Hercules and Montedison dominates, even if they remain competitors in the background. The parents are not effectively assured of the joint venture's control. Keeping such an operation outside the scope of Article 85(1) is not conceptually wrong, even if this scope were to be extended to the control of certain mergers. It suffices then to complete the analysis by an examination of the case from that angle. In the Himont case the application of Article 86 was examined but considered unjustified. A double test of the applicability of Article 85(1) would have led to the same result.

---

[31] IP (87) 128 of 26 March 1987.

6. Conclusion

The debate on the balance between competition and co-operation on the Common Market is far from over,[32] in particular where co-operation is intensified and strengthened by capital participation, i.e. by joint ventures. In a realistic approach without preconceived ideas and interest-orientated consideration it is obvious that public and private interests do not really conflict in the matter, provided neither side exaggerated. Joint ventures cannot be considered as restrictive *per se*. All that is needed is adequate public control over those joint ventures that reduce the stimulus of competition below the level required for the proper functioning of the Common Market.

It is submitted that such public control results from the administrative practice of the Commission, as summarized above. Enterprise in general disposes of considerable possibilities for non-restrictive co-operation. Small and medium firms benefit moreover from considerable liberty for restrictive co-operation, provided certain quantitative and qualitative criteria are met. Market entry requirements, rationalization objectives and market exit situations equally have many possibilities to remain outside Article 85(1), provided firms resist the temptation to regulate more than is strictly and objectively necessary for the type of operation envisaged. In the remaining domain, individual exemptions are far from excluded.

It is also submitted that in this approach the requirements of public control – administrative or judicial – are reduced to manageable proportions. True, the correct application of the procedures of Regulation 17 continues to cause delays which are not really compatible with industries' need for co-operation. In this respect further improvement should be sought, if necessary, through a modification of Regulation 17, which is anyhow in need of modernisation.

The nullity which Article 85(2) attaches to joint venture agreements which infringe Article 85(1) and which are not exempted or exemptible, should be jealously preserved. More particularly the temptation should be resisted to deal with joint-ventures under a future merger regulation which may be adopted in 1988 if present optimistic expectations become reality. This temptation may well be felt because according to the present draft[33] transactions coming within the ambit of this regulation will not be automatically null and void, but will give rise to an order of separation or cessation of common control.

The nullity of restrictive agreements or practices is a powerful weapon of

---

[32] An even more recent Article 19(3) notice concerns an existing joint venture between Bayer and BP, the distribution of the products of the joint venture and the building of a new plant. (OJ 1987 C 253, p. 5.)

[33] OJ 1973 C 92, p. 1 *ff.* art. 3.2.

public control. To renounce this weapon in respect of joint ventures would be a major retreat, for which there is no convincing justification in law. The ECSC precedent[34] – joint ventures between ECSC enterprises have been brought under Article 66 ECSC – should not be overestimated. The requirements of an industrial sector in decline may be satisfied by that interpretation but this does not justify, by itself, the extension of this interpretation to a competition policy, that covers the whole spectrum of economic activities and all phases of the economic cycle. For that purpose a different balance of power between public control and co-operation in joint ventures is needed.

In this respect it should be recalled that according to Article 66(5) ECSC the granting of export approval of a merger that did not obtain an *a priori* authorization, is subject to the payment of substantial fines. A similar provision is lacking in the draft regulation on merger control in the EEC domain. Moreover, notification will only be obligatory for big mergers. As a result the position of the Commission, under future EEC rules will be considerably weaker than under ECSC rules. A difference of this kind also pleads against the extension of future EEC merger control to joint ventures.

In this author's view, the better solution for joint ventures resides in the rapid adoption of a clear and comprehensible overview of the state of the law on joint ventures under Article 85, drafted in a manner which allowes industry to use the instrument of co-operative deployment of production factors in a manner which minimizes the need for public control. The sooner guidelines of that type are available, the better competition and co-operation will develop.

---

[34] *See* Ritter in Langen, Kartellgesetz par. I No. EG 146.

VII. Industrial restructuring operations and EEC competition law

R.H. LAUWAARS

1. Introduction

Today's European industry is characterised by a process of permanent adaptation. On the one hand it has to prepare itself for the completion of the internal market in 1992. On the other hand it has to defend and, if possible, to strengthen its position on a world market where it is confronted with severe competition, in particular from enterprises of the other industrial superpowers.

Under such circumstances enterprises look for co-operation with others. This co-operation may relate to certain entrepreneurial activities, as R & D, which, if carried out jointly, may enable the participating undertakings to enter into R & D-projects, which exceed the financial resources of each of them individually. However, in certain sectors, especially those which are in difficulties, co-operation goes further. In these cases co-operation may lead to a comprehensive restructuring of activities, which may be defined as the transfer of ownership of certain production facilities in order to increase the competitiveness of each of the participating undertakings or agreements which, although they do not provide for an immediate transfer of ownership, aim at the same objective.

This article discusses the above-mentioned industrial restructuring operations and their compatibility with the competition law of the EEC. First of all the actual practice of the Commission in this field will be treated (para. 2). Secondly, the advantages and disadvantages of this practice will be mentioned (para. 3). Finally, some remarks will be made about the possible removal of the drawbacks and in particular about the fundamental problem which is raised by the assessment of restructuring, *i.e.* the relationship between competition policy and industrial policy (para. 4).

2. Practice of the Commission

Leaving aside the abortive attempt of ICI and Montedison to establish and exploit a joint venture for the production of nitrobenzene and aniline,[1] the

---

[1] Bull. EC 1977/7–8, pp. 30–32 (para. 2.1.31).

Commission's practice started in 1983 and has been laid down in formal as well as informal pronouncements.[2]

A. Rovin[3]

Rovin is a joint venture established by Akzo Zout Chemie Nederland BV and Shell Nederland Chemie BV. It embodies an integrated production process for vinyl chloride monomer (VCM) and polyvinyl chloride (PVC) and aims at achieving a structural improvement of capacity utilization. For that purpose one party (Shell) will put its PVC plant at the disposal of the joint venture, and the other (Akzo) its VCM plant. Through the production capacity which is thus made available to the joint venture, the parties will produce for it PVC, VCM or ethylene dichloride (EDC) in such quantities and of such quality as specified in a co-operation agreement, using the prime materials which they deliver to the joint venture.

This agreement and the adjoining agreements relating to the same subject have been found by the Commission to be acceptable. In the Bulletin it is stated that 'measures to ensure fuller use of capacity may be authorized under certain conditions, provided there are no unacceptable restrictions on competition, such as price-fixing or the allocation of quotas'.[4]

Rovin is the first case where the Commission admitted a restructuring operation in the chemical industry. At the same time, it is the first application of the Commission's practice to close its file by means of a so-called 'provisional letter', *i.e.* a letter from the Director-General for Competition stating that the Directorate-General for Competition does not consider it necessary to pursue the formal procedure through to the adoption of a Decision under Article 85, para. 3, but with the reservation that the file will be re-opened in the event of a change in the factual or legal situation.[5] According to the Commission's Notice about these letters the essential contents of the notified agreements will first be published in the Official Journal by virtue of Article 19, para. 3, Regulation No. 17.[6] The same Notice stipulates that a 'list of the cases dealt with by dispatch of provisional letters following publication will be appended to the Report on Competition Policy'.[7]

---

[2] In describing the Commission's practice we will mainly focus upon the Commission's formal and informal decision-making in respect of the chemical industry.

[3] OJ 1983, C 295/7 (notice) and Bull. EC 1984/5, pp. 37–38. (para. 2.1.47).

[4] Note 3 *supra*, at 38.

[5] *See* Notice from the Commission on procedures concerning notifications pursuant to Article 4 of Council Regulation No. 17/62, OJ 1983, C 295/6, and *Thirteenth Report on Competition Policy (1983)*, nr. 72.

[6] *See* as to Rovin, OJ 1983, C 295/7.

[7] *See* for Rovin: *Fourteenth Report on Competition Policy (1984)*, Annex, at 231, under the heading 'Administrative letters sent following publication of a notice pursuant to Article 19 (3) of Regulation No. 17'.

Since these 'provisional letters' embodied a new simplified procedure which could in principle also be applied to other restructuring operations, we would like to make two additional comments. It has in the first place to be observed that they have been used in a very limited number of cases only. Although they have been sent in a number of cases after Rovin,[8] these cases had nothing to do with restructuring and in general one could say that the practical meaning of the 'provisional letters' is relatively modest. Secondly, these 'provisional letters' should be distinguished from the so-called 'comfort letters', as mentioned in OJ 1982, C 343/4. A 'comfort letter' establishes the inapplicability of Article 85, para. 1 and may therefore be considered as a 'quasi negative clearance'.[9] In this case, too, the essential contents of the agreement are published in the Official Journal; cases which are closed by way of a comfort letter will subsequently be mentioned in the Official Journal.[10] Van Bael/Bellis refer to both letters as 'comfort letters', making a distinction between 'comfort letters' in the old style, *i.e.* without any publicity, and 'comfort letters' in the new style, *i.e.* with publication of the essential contents of the agreement in the OJ, information of the Advisory Committee and listing in the Annual Report on Competition Policy.[11] Bellamy and Child make a distinction between 'comfort letters' and 'formal comfort letters'. The first are granted without any publicity; the second cover 'comfort letters' and 'provisional letters' as well.[12] However, in our view, these authors do not stress sufficiently that 'comfort letters' contain a declaration of inapplicability of Article 85, *as such* and 'provisional letters' are a mere 'stop' half-way on the road to a formal exemption.

B.   BP Chemicals Ltd./ICI

In a Decision of 19 July 1984[13] the Commission granted an exemption in respect of a number of agreements concluded between British Petroleum Chemicals Ltd. (BPCL) and Imperial Chemical Industries (ICI) regarding a restructuring in the British petro-chemical industry. These agreements provided for the mutual sale of certain production units and connected goodwill as well as the mutual grant of patent and know-how licences for PVC and LDPE respectively ('low-density polyethylene'). BPCL bought the LDPE-business and ICI the PVC-business. Each of the parties moreover closed

---

[8]   Examples are: Kathon Biocide, OJ 1984, C 59/6; BBC/Grenfell/Holt, OJ 1984, C 209/3; VFA/Sauer, OJ 1985, C 68/2; ICL/Fujitsu, OJ 1986, C 210/3, and ARG/Unipart, OJ 1986, C 319/3.

[9]   *See* e.g. the notice regarding 'Europages', OJ 1982, C 343/5.

[10] *See* OJ 1982, C 343/4.

[11] Competition Law of the EEC (CCH Editions Ltd., Bicester, 1987), pp. 318–320.

[12] Common Market Law of Competition, 3rd ed. (London, 1987), paras. 11–004, 11–070 and 11–071.

[13] OJ 1984, L 212/1.

down its production units for LDPE and PVC respectively which were not involved in the agreements, be it that ICI would still have two LDPE plants on the Continent.

According to the Commission the agreements plus the associated closure of plants ultimately had the same result as a *specialization agreement* and an agreement to limit capacity. It further held that the sale of both the plants and the goodwill effectively precluded BPCL and ICI respectively from competing with the purchaser and *implicitly forced* them to close the remaining units (paras. 26.1 and 26.2). Both parties were, in the Commission's view, still potential competitors and it denied that the agreements could be qualified as a 'partial concentration/merger' which would be outside the scope of Article 85, para. 1 (para. 31).[14] The Commission granted an exemption, because 'the closures of the older plants reduced capacities in sectors which were suffering from structural overcapacity'.[15] In that connection the Commission explicitly referred to the Rovin case and observed that the present case, too, fitted in with its policy on measures to reduce industrial overcapacity.

C. ENI/Montedison

In a Decision of 4 December 1986[16] the Commission further granted an exemption for a large restructuring operation between the Italian companies Ente Nazionale Idrocarburi (ENI) and Montedison.

The operation consisted of a set of agreements under which the parties transferred to one another part of their basic chemicals and thermo-plastics businesses and a number of further agreements concerning supply and plant operation arrangements and licensing of patents and know-how. The Decision also concerned agreements about the closure, capacity reduction and conversion of certain plants or facilities.

ENI is the Italian-state holding company for the energy sector (Enichem is its subsidiary for petrochemicals), Montedison is a diversified privately-owned Italian group of companies. The products concerned by the agreements are all derivatives of naphta, the basic feedstock used in the European petrochemical industry. The Commission mentions that the markets for these products are characterized by structural overcapacity, which in Italy led to the establishment of a Government rationalization plan (the 'Chemical Plan'), the centrepiece of which was formed by the present agreements.

---

[14] The Commission stated that the agreements went far beyond a 'simple partial concentration' and added that the 'foregoing is without prejudice to the question whether such a concentration would justify the non-application of Article 85(1)' (para. 31). *See* about the latter point the judgment of the Court of 17 November 1987 in Joined Cases 142 and 156/84 (*B.A.T. and Reynolds vs. Commission*).
[15] Bull. EC 1984/7–8, p. 31 (para. 2.1.55).
[16] OJ 1987, L 5/13.

The basic agreement involved the reciprocal transfer of certain lines of business and all fixed and intangible assets and resulted, according to the Commission, to a *de facto specialization*. ENI obtained a part of the cracking business of Montedison (ethylene and other naphta derivatives) as well as production facilities for LDPE and similar products. Montedison obtained the polypropylene – and polystyrene – business from ENI and a sum in cash. The agreements concerning supply and plant operation arrangements relate to plants which would in the future be partly owned by one party and partly by the other. The whole set of agreements contained also certain *no-competition clauses* for a period of five years and provided the parties with the possibility to slim down certain consolidated businesses (para. 13).

According to the Commission, the whole set of agreements contained the following restrictions of competition:

(i) Specialization (because it leads to a sharing of markets which has been made legally binding by the reciprocal non-competition clauses);
(ii) reduction of capacity (agreements between competitors designed to close plants and limit capacity, by their very nature, have a direct effect on competition); and
(iii) the necessity for continued co-operation between actual or potential competitors.

The Commission denied (again) that the agreements could be qualified as 'simple assets transfers' outside the scope of Article 85, para. 1 (para. 22). The agreements did, however, meet the conditions for exemption. The main reason for this view was that the agreements were an 'essential first step' in the rationalization of ENI's and Montedison's petrochemical business 'which forms part of an industry suffering serious structural overcapacity in the whole Community'. The agreements thus produce 'objective benefits' which outweigh the abovementioned restrictions of competition. (paras. 27 en 28).

D.   Montedison/Hercules (Himont)

Within the framework of its informal competition policy the Commission authorized the establishment by Montedison and Hercules of the company Himont.[17] This company is established in the USA. It obtained the assets of both parent companies in the polypropylene sector. According to the original agreements Himont should be involved in the production of polypropylene resins (a semi-manufacture) and polypropylene fibres; sales would be effectuated by subsidiaries of Himont or of one of the parent companies.

Under the same agreements Montedison and Hercules would remain

---

[17] Bull. EC 1987/3, pp. 32–33 (para. 2.1.71).

active in the production and sale of polypropylene film; Montedison would continue its production of propylene and Hercules its production of poly-propylene fibres in the USA. The three companies would buy minimum quantities of their requirements of polypropylene resins or propylene from one another at relatively cheap prices. Finally, Himont was set up as a 50/50 joint venture.

All these clauses were, however, in the Commission's view incompatible with Article 85, para. 1. In that connection it referred in particular to both Hercules' and Montedison's presence in the polypropylene film sector, which is one of Himont's downstream markets, to Hercules' presence in the polypropylene fiber market in the USA and to Montedison's presence in Himont's upstream market, propylene. It further raised objections against the special supply and purchasing agreements; the distribution of Himont's products by Hercules and Montedison, and the fact that joint control over Himont was strictly shared between the two parents.

To meet these objections it has now been stipulated that 20% of Himont's common stock will be sold on the Stock Exchange. Hercules and Montedison will further withdraw from the downstream market of Himont in the Community (polypropylene film). Himont has given up all its interests in the polypropylene fibre sector and will itself take care of the marketing of its products in the major Member States. The special supply and purchasing agreements have been terminated. Under those circumstances the agreements on Himont fall outside the scope of Article 85, para. 1.

The Commission stated that the parent companies have withdrawn 'com-pletely and permanently' from the market of the joint venture, with the exception of certain activities 'on a very small scale'. There was no ground to apply Article 86.

E.   Enichem/ICI

The Official Journal of 15 August 1987[18] further contains a Notice concern-ing a series of agreements between Enichem and ICI on the establishment of a joint venture, European Vinyls Corporation (EVC), which will operate in the VCM and PVC sectors. A supplement to these agreements extends the co-operation to PVC primary and secondary plasticizers. The agreements cover Enichem's and ICI's interests in VCM and all forms of PVC as well as certain EDC manufacturing plants that are closely associated with VCM manufacture (para. 4).

The Commission observes that many sectors of the petrochemical industry are still suffering from structural overcapacity and that the producers 'have been forced to look for ways of reducing their capacity either by individual

---

[18] OJ 1987, C 217/2.

closures or through bilateral deals with other producers'. Both Enichem and ICI are now in the 'second round of restructuring', having already rationalized capacity in other sectors in swap deals with Montedison and BP respectively which were approved by the Commission (see sub (c) and (b) respectively, *supra*).

EVC is set up as a 50/50 joint venture to produce and sell the products mentioned above. It is to operate for at least five years from 1 October 1986 (para. 6). The aim of Enichem and ICI in setting up EVC is to complete the restructuring of their VCM/PVC business in order to regain competitiveness and to reduce losses (para. 12). The agreements also provide for *plant closures*, which together amount to over half of the total estimated surplus capacity in the VCM/PVC sector in Western Europe in 1986 (para. 13). The Commission intends to grant an exemption for five years on condition, *inter alia*, that the parties do not extend their cooperation to include other companies (para. IV).

F. Bayer/BP

Finally, the Official Journal of 23 September 1987[19] contains a Notice concerning a series of agreements between Bayer AG, BP Chemicals Int. Ltd. (BP) and Erdölchemie GmbH (EC) in the polyethylene sector; under these agreements BP is appointed as distributor for EC's production and technical co-operation is established between BP and EC. The latter company is a joint venture of Deutsche BP AG and Bayer. All its products are currently distributed by Bayer (para. 2). The purpose of the agreements is to appoint BP as distributor of EC's products instead of Bayer. Futhermore, BP will grant EC its polyethylene (LdPE and LLdPE) process technology.[20] As to this point BP and Bayer have agreed to build a new LLdPE plant at EC's premises in Cologne-Worringen (para. 6, sub (a)).

The Commission holds (again) that the case concerns a 'second round of restructuring', namely in respect of BP which had already rationalized capacity through the swap deal with ICI (sub (b), *supra*). When BP is going to distribute also the LdPE produced by EC, it will become the largest supplier of this product in the Community. In this case, too, the Commission proposes to grant an exemption, on condition, *inter alia*, that the parties fully implement the proposed industrial restructuring changes. The parties will moreover be required to inform the Commission in advance of any further operation in the LdPE/LLdPE sector in which they intend to take part (para. IV).

---

[19] OJ 1987, C 253/5.
[20] 'LdPE' and 'LLdPE' stand for resp. low density polyethylene and linear low density polyethylene.

3. Advantages and disadvantages of the Commission's actual practice

As may have appeared from the above, the Commission has adopted a positive attitude towards restructuring operations in the West European chemical industry.[21] Already in its Twelfth Report on Competition Policy (1982), the Commission stated that 'it is up to each undertaking to assess for itself whether and at which point (structural) overcapacity becomes economically unsustainable and to take the necessary measures to reduce it'.[22] Against this background the Commission might be able to condone agreements in restraint of competition which relate to a *sector as a whole*, provided they are aimed solely at achieving a co-ordinated reduction of overcapacity and do not otherwise restrict free decision-making by the firms involved. The necessary structural reorganization must not be achieved by 'unsuitable means' such as price-fixing, quota arrangements or market-sharing.[23] Do these statements relate to so-called crisis cartels – a subject that is not discussed in this article – the same considerations apply to *bilateral agreements*. 'As an alternative to such sectoral agreements, the Commission can also envisage agreements between a small number of firms providing for reciprocal specialization which would enable them to close excess capacity'.[24] In both cases the number of Community producers left has to be sufficient to maintain effective competition in the Community.[25] This view has been confirmed by the Thirteenth Report on Competition Policy (1983). The Commission repeats that in its view 'reciprocal specialization agreements to close excess capacity' are an alternative to sectoral arrangements. Rovin is mentioned as an example.[26]

However, the actual practice of the Commission is not without certain drawbacks:

(i) *Length of the procedure:* Taking the date of notification as our starting point, the decision-making procedure in the present cases had the following duration:

Rovin: less than 1.5 year (notification on 30 September 1983; information about the authorization in the Bulletin of May 1984);

BP Chemicals/ICI: 1.5 year (notification on 28 January 1983; exemption on 19 July 1984);

ENI/Montedison: 3 years (notification on 19 October 1983; exemption on 4 December 1986).[27]

---

[21] As confirmed by Mr Sutherland in his speech for the Kangaroo Group about 'The Question of Mergers: What Should Be Done?', Antwerp, 2 Nov. 1987, at 14.

[22] *Twelfth Report on Competition Policy* (1983), nr. 38.

[23] *Ibid.*, nr. 39, as supplemented by Thirteenth Report on Competition Policy (1984), nr. 56.

[24] *Twelfth Report*, nr. 40.

[25] *Ibid.*, nr. 41.

[26] *Thirteenth Report on Competition Policy* (1984), nr. 60.

[27] The report in the Bulletin 1987/3 about Montedison/Hercules does not give information about this. The Notices concerning resp. Enichem/ICI and Bayer/BP are just announcements of the Commission's intention to grant an exemption. They appeared respectively 1.5 and 1 year after the date of notification.

Although objectively, *i.e.* compared with the length of the decision-making procedure in other cases, these periods are short, they are too long for the kind of operations under discussion. If anywhere then certainly here the phrase applies that the iron shoud be struck while it is hot, which means that a restructuring operation, once agreed, should get its seal under competition law as soon as possible. The parties should, therefore, obtain within a short time legal certainty about the validity of their agreements. The 'provisional letter', mentioned in para. II, sub (a), is a very laudable attempt to accelerate procedures, but it does not offer complete legal certainty.[28]

(ii) Period of exemption: This is the second 'time-problem': exemptions are – and by virtue of Article 8, para. 1, Regulation No. 17 may only be – granted for a 'specified period'. Thus, the exemptions *in re* BP Chemicals/ICI and ENI/Montedison respectively have been granted for 15 years (from the date of notification). The Notice concerning Enichem/ICI mentions a period of five years. However, such a time limit is hard to reconcile with the character of a restructuring operation as a permanent modification; it seems to be inappropriate and diminishes legal security, when this has been obtained.

(iii) Conditions and obligations: According to the same Article 8, para. 1, of Regulation No. 17 exemptions 'may' contain conditions and obligations. This possibility is not left by the Commission unused. So it has been stipulated in the Decision BP Chemicals/ICI that ICI, beyond the period necessary to transfer the value of the goodwill and assimilate the technology (four years), shall transmit a three yearly report about its sales (and those of its associated companies and subsidiaries) of LDPE in the UK as well as a breakdown of sales by status of purchaser; the report should also mention its total LDPE-production. BP Chemicals is under a similar obligation in respect of PVC, if it or any associated company or subsidiary ever acquires any PVC production facilities in Europe or any other area from which imports into the UK could be viably made. Both parties have to inform the Commission forthwith of any amendments or additions to the agreements.

From the long list of obligations contained in the Decision ENI/Montedison we mention the obligation of ENI and Montedison respectively to submit to the Commission three-yearly reports about production and sales of the products which have been 'assigned' to each of them in the common market as a whole and in each Member State as well as total production of each of those products in the EEC and in other countries. Each party shall further inform the Commission in advance of any further operation in which it, or its subsidiaries or associated companies, will take part.

The conditions and obligations which the Commission intends to impose in the Enichem/ICI and Bayer/BP Cases have already been mentioned above (para. 2, sub (e) and (f), *supra*).

---

[28] *See* about the possible binding effect of a provisional letter: Van Bael/Bellis, note 11 *supra*, p. 319.

The difficulty with these provisions is that they are a heavy burden for the participating undertakings, which – again – does not fit in with the permanent structural modification aimed at.

It may appear from the above that the applicable rules are not perfectly suited to cover the kind of operations under discussion. In order to bring them nevertheless within the scope of the rules, the latter had to be applied with a certain artificiality, for example by qualifying a swap arrangement as a 'reciprocal specialization agreement to close excess capacity'.[29] However, according to Article 1(a) of Regulation No. 417/85,[30] a specialization agreement is an agreement whereby, for the duration of the agreement, undertakings accept reciprocal obligations 'not to manufacture certain products or to have them manufactured, but to leave it to other parties to manufacture the products or have them manufactured'. The Article seems to presuppose that each of the parties retains its own production capacity and will be prepared, by virtue of mutual obligations of exclusive supply, to continue the sale of the specialized products.[31] Thus, in BP Chemicals/ICI the Commission holds that the final result of the swap agreements (plus the associated plant closures) 'is equivalent to' both a production specialization agreement and an agreement to limit capacity.[32] And in ENI/Montedison it is said that the reciprocal asset swaps result in a 'de facto specialization' accompanied by concerted action to reduce capacity.[33]

4. Removal of the drawbacks: the draft merger control regulation and the co-ordination of competition policy and industrial policy

The most straightforward solution to the problems which have been raised, would be the adoption by the Council of the draft regulation on the control of mergers. The draft has already been submitted by the Commission in 1973;[34] since 1980 it has been changed three times.[35] Although, during many years, the Council was unable to overcome its internal disagreement, recently the situation has fundamentally changed. On 30 November 1987, the Council in principle accepted the idea of merger control; ten countries fully supported the Commission's position, while two (France and the UK) expressed reservations.[36]

---

[29] *Thirteenth Report*, nr. 60.
[30] Commission Regulation (EEC) No. 417/85 of 19 December 1984, OJ 1985, L 53/1, on the application of Article 85(3) of the Treaty to categories of specialization agreements.
[31] *First Report on Competition Policy* (1971), nr. 27.
[32] Note 13 *supra*, para. 26, opening words.
[33] Note 16 *supra*, para. 22, sub (iv).
[34] OJ 1973, C 92/1.
[35] *See* OJ 1982, C 36/3; 1984, C 51/8, and 1986, C 324/5.
[36] *Agence Europe* No. 4671 of 2 December 1987, p. 5.

According to Article 1, para. 1, of the draft, as amended, direct or indirect concentrations, which provide the undertakings involved with the power 'to hinder effective competition in the common market or in a substantial part thereof, (are) incompatible with the common market'. A concentration shall, however, be presumed to be compatible with the common market where the market share of the goods or services concerned accounts in the common market or in a substantial part thereof, for less than 20% of the turnover in identical or similar goods or services. The prohibition does not apply where the aggregate turnover of the participating undertakings is less than 750 million Ecu (Article 1, para. 2). The provisions of para. 1 may further be declared inapplicable to concentrations which are indispensable to the attainment of a priority of the Community (Article 1, para. 3).

Concentrations between undertakings, the total turnover of which is 1,000 million Ecu or more must be notified before they are put into effect (Article 4, para. 1). As regards concentrations notified to it, the Commission shall commence proceedings within a period of three months (Article 6, para. 2); otherwise the concentration shall be presumed to be compatible with the common market (para. 4). A decision prohibiting or authorizing a concentration shall be taken within nine months following the date of the initiation of the procedure (Article 17, para. 1 (a)).

Shortly before the Council meeting, referred to above, the idea of European Merger Control had also been supported by UNICE.[37] In its Declaration it is stressed that the control mechanism should enable companies to take rapid decisions; such a system of European Merger Control will also remove the second drawback of the actual practice of the Commission (limited validity of an exemption). As to our third point (the excessive number of conditions and obligations) the present draft stipulates that the Commission may attach conditions and obligations to its authorizing decision (Article 3, para. 4). It remains to be seen what use the Commission will make of this power, assuming that it will be maintained in this form in the final text of the Regulation. The most important point is, however, that the Regulation should have *exclusive effect*, *i.e.* that mergers and merger-like operations like the ones under discussion which come within the scope of the Regulation, should no longer be subjected to national controls and neither be judged under Article 85 or 86.

Much will depend on the amendments which the Commission will make to its original proposal and on the negotiations in the Council. However, instead of speculating about their possible outcome, we would like to make some final remarks about the underlying fundamental problem which is the relationship between competition and industrial policies. In his speech at the

---

[37] Union of Industrial and Employers Confederations of Europe, 'Merger Control at Community Level', Declaration of 10 November 1987.

Kangaroo Group Conference on 2 November 1987 about 'The Question of Mergers: What Should be Done?' Commissioner Sutherland approached this subject as follows:

'Indeed, the Commission's competition policy cannot be encapsulated by the sole objective of removing distortions caused by anti-trust practices or state aids which are liable to interfere with inter-state trade. Competition policy also contributes to improving the allocation of resources and raising the competitiveness of Community industry and thanks to this greater competitiveness, secured largely by encouragement of research and development, to enable the Community ultimately to overcome its economic problems, and in particular to combat structural unemployment. In this way competition policy can play its part, alongside other Community policies, in promoting economic growth'.

'Some of our industries are in decline. Some of our new industries are rapidly growing. An open internal market will increase the necessity of a coherent industrial policy at Community level. In the long term it must be possible for industrial restructuring to take place smoothly. That is why within the framework of competition policy, the Commission takes a positive approach towards programmes of industrial restructuring.'[38]

In our view, this means *in concreto* that two objectives have to be reconciled: on the one hand, the maintenance of effective competition within the common market and, on the other hand, the improvement of the competitive strength of the undertakings, also – and not the least – on the world market. This means that in the case a restructuring operation would be prohibited on grounds of competition policy (because it would lower the degree of competition below the level of effectiveness), other, industrial policy measures should be taken to cope with the economic difficulties the restructuring was meant to solve. The relationship between competition policy and industrial policy is, however, a *two-way-street*. In its turn competition policy should take account of the objectives of industrial policy.

In 1981 the Commission added to Article 1, para. 1, second subparagraph of the draft Regulation, that the power to hinder effective competition should also be assessed with reference to 'the effects of international competition'. In 1984 this was changed into 'international competition'. According to the Explanatory Note these words were added to make it clear that account must be taken of the 'competitive situation and the development of trade at international level'.[39] Mergers and merger-like operations will, therefore, have to be judged in the light of the global competitive framework. Decisions about the 'maintenance of the effective competition within the common market' will not only have to take account of the competition by undertakings in third countries on the European market, but also with

---

[38] Note 21 *supra*, at 14.
[39] OJ 1982, C 36/3, sub II. a.

the necessity to increase the competitiveness of European companies on the world market.[40] It is arguable that in the utmost case, *i.e.* when the objectives of competition policy and those of industrial policy are irreconcilable, industrial policy considerations should be the determinative factor.

---

[40] *Cf.* Art. 130F new of the EEC Treaty which stipulates that one of the Community's aims is to encourage European industry 'to become more competitive at international level', and, previously, recital 10 of the Preamble to Reg. No. 418/85 on the application of Article 85(3) of the Treaty to categories of R & D agreements, OJ 1985, L 53/5 ('world competition' as a ground for the granting of an individual exemption to an agreement which does not fulfil the market share conditions of the Regulation).

VIII.   Licensing competitors

WILLY ALEXANDER

1.   Introduction

The present contribution is devoted to an analysis of EEC competition policy in respect of the licensing of technology.

It is limited to those patent licensing agreements and know-how agreement which may have effects on competition either between licensor and licensees or between licensees or between licensees and third parties. Statements of civil servants of the Commission confirm my impression that the overwhelming part of patent licence agreements have so-called horizontal effects.[1]

2.   Competition protected by Article 85

A.   Abstractions

In spite of all statements that EEC competition law does not employ *per se* rules, its application shows a very high degree of abstraction with almost similar effects. The treatment of patent licences is an example of this approach.

EEC competition policy in this field started by the publication in 1962 of a list of clauses which, in the view of the Commission, would not be caught by the prohibition of Article 85(1).[2] This announcement was only withdrawn in 1984 in exchange of a regulation exempting, under Article 85(3), all patent licensing agreements which satisfy certain conditions.[3] Moreover, Article 3 of that regulation contains a list of clauses which are considered by patentees and licensees, and probably not without reason, as being practically *per se* prohibited. Nowhere, in any of these statements,

---

[1] Johannes, 'Technology Transfer under EEC Law – Europe between the Divergent Opinions of the Past and New Administration: A Comparative Law Approach', in Annual Proceedings of Fordham Corp. L. Inst. (1983), 65, at 83–84; Van der Esch, 'Industrial Property Rights under EEC Law', in Annual Proceedings of Fordham Corp. L. Inst. (1984), 539, at 549.

[2] Commission, Notice on Patent Licensing Agreements, OJ 24 December 1962, p. 2922.

[3] Commission, Regulation No. 2349/84 on the application of Article 85(3) of the Treaty to certain categories of patents licensing agreements, OJ 16 August 1984 No L 219/15.

reference is made to elements like the importance of the parties and of the licensed technology.

So far for the form of the policy. The reasoning of the 1962 announcement was, itself, based on theoretical principles. The main one was inspired by § 20(1) of the German Act against Restraints of Competition. It implied that certain obligations could not restrict competition within the meaning of Article 85(1), because they are 'covered by the patent', because they 'entail only the partial maintenance of the right of prohibition contained in the patentee's exclusive right in relation to the licensee'.

It is not clear whether the withdrawal by the Commission of its 1962 announcement marks its real abandonment of this type of theories.

The Court of Justice has, in its case law relating to the free movement of goods, introduced the term 'specific subject matter of the industrial property', which it has also applied to Article 85.

Article 30 of the Treaty prohibits quantitative restrictions on imports as between Member States and all measures having equivalent effect; Article 36 adds that this shall not preclude prohibitions or restrictions on imports justified on the grounds of the protection of industrial property. The Court has ruled that an exercise of patent rights which would prevent the marketing of goods imported from another Member State is caught by the prohibition of Article 30, but may rely on the exception of Article 36 if it is necessary 'for the purpose of safeguarding rights which constitute the specific subject matter of this property'. In relation to patents, this specific subject matter is the guarantee that the patentee, to reward the creative effort of the inventor, has the exclusive right to use an invention with a view to manufacturing industrial products and putting them into circulation for the first time, either directly or by the grant of licences to third parties, as well as the right to oppose infringements.[4] The practical result has been that preventing imports from other Member States is legal if the product has been manufactured there by an independent third party without the consent of the owner of the patent which is invoked.[5]

The Court's definition of the subject matter of the patent may not be free from criticism. Nevertheless, some general yardstick such as developed by the Court appears to be necessary in order to distinguish legal obstacles to imports from illegal ones.

The Court has extended the same terminology to the realm of Article 85(1). In *Windsurfing International*, it declared that an obligation on the licensee to affix a notice stating 'licensed by ...' may be 'covered by the specific subject matter of the patent' and that the obligation not to challenge the validity of the licensed patent clearly does not fall 'within the specific

---

[4] Case 15/74, Sterling Drug, 31 October 1974, ECR 1974, page 1147.
[5] Case 15/74, Sterling Drug, 31 October 1974, ECR 1974, page 1147; Case 187/80 Merck, 14 July 1981, ECR 1981, p. 2063; Case 19/84 Pharmon, 9 July 1985, not yet reported.

subject matter of the patent'. With respect to the no-challenge clause the Court added that it is in the public interest to eliminate any obstacle to economic activity which may arise where a patent was granted in error. But the Court's analysis of the clause concerning the notice suggests that the question whether it has as its object or effect the prevention, restriction or distortion of competition only arises if the clause is not covered by the 'specific subject matter of the patent'.[6]

My objection against abstract and vague criteria, as those mentioned above, lies in the fact that they are not based on a determination of the type of competition which Article 85(1) seeks to protect and that they may, consequently, conceal important issues.

On the other hand, once these issues have been analyzed and solved, an easy administration of the law and legal security afford grounds for listing specific clauses which should generally be avoided or which are generally acceptable. The means for such a policy are created by Regulation no. 19/65,[7] which is the legal basis for block exemptions in respect of patent licensing agreements and know-how agreements.

B.   The choice between competition and cooperation

The general attitude towards licensing has always been a favorable one. In the light of the mechanism of Article 85 it is expressed by the use of two successive steps. The first one says that granting licences falls, in principle, outside the scope of Article 85(1). This prohibition can only be applicable on account of particular clauses or factual circumstances. The second way is a declaration that, even then, they have a good chance of being exempted under Article 85(3), except for certain clauses or situations.

All this – the favorable attitude and the high degree of abstraction – is satisfactory for licensing parties and their advisors. But to what extent does the policy, as developed so far, reflect conscious choices?

These choices should involve, on the one hand, an identification of the various aspects of competition which may be concerned, and, on the other hand, a determination whether the advantages of certain licensing agreements compensate for the negative effects on competition.

In assessing the restrictive effects of distribution agreements, a distinction is made between effects on intra-brand competition and those on inter-brand competition. In the same vein a distinction can be made between the effects of licensing agreements on competition within the licensed technology (intra-technology competition) and on competition between technologies (inter-technology competition).

---

[6] Case 193/83, Windsurfing International, 25 February 1986, ECR 1986, page 611.
[7] OJ 6 March 1965, p. 533.

C. Competition within a licensed technology

The old theory that certain restrictions in licensing agreements are inherent in the patent monopoly and therefore do not constitute restrictions of competition, is based on the assumption that the patentee is free to determine the degree to which he makes his exclusive technology accessible to outsiders. That is begging the question.

If something may be called inherent in the patent monopoly, it is the prospect of monopoly rents, which constitutes the incentive by means of which patent acts seek to make research and development, the publication of their results and investment in their application attractive. What should be respected by competition policy is the choice of the owner of the technology between exploiting it through retaining his exclusivity of manufacture and sale or by allowing other manufacturers to share the technology.

By exposing operators to enhanced competition, Article 85(1) seeks to attain objectives, like optimal allocation of resources, increased efficiency and the search of new markets, which are not less applicable to licensors and licensees of technology. As a matter of principle, there is no reason to treat their agreements differently from other transactions in respect of material or immaterial goods.

Of course, there may be reasons for competition policy to make licensing more attractive to the owners of the technology or to make it attractive for potential licensees to seek a licence. Such considerations may justify a lenient attitude towards moderation of competition between manufacturers operating within a licensed technology. But this is a matter which falls within the framework of Article 85(3).

D. Competition between different technologies

Competition between different technologies or innovative competition is a concept that requires more study. At present, I would limit myself to a few remarks.

This type of competition certainly has many aspects. One can think of the effort of circumventing an existing patent, of the race between various systems for the conquest of a new market (as in the case of video-recording) or of the use of a licensed technology as a take-off run for independent innovation (like in post-war Japan).

Regard for innovative competition would lead to considering the significance of the technology and the importance of the contracting parties and of outsiders, in assessing licensing agreements.

This may lead to a negative assessment. It may, e.g., be based on doubt whether a contracting party, which already occupies a dominant or important position in the technology at issue, should be allowed to acquire a certain licence or future improvements.

But is may also lead to a positive view. It can find its origin in the public interest in a larger diffusion of a certain innovation or in standardization of elements of a technology. It may also be justified by a need for lifting a stalemate resulting from conflicting patents, or for increasing the competitiveness of certain firms *vis-à-vis* a powerful firm or on the world market.

3. EEC Policy in Concreto

A. Quantitative importance

Present EEC policy in respect of licensing of patents and of ancillary know-how has found expression in the form of ten formal decisions, two of which were reviewed by the Court of Justice,[8] some publications in the Annual Reports on Competition Policy concerning informal settlements and the block exemption for patent licensing agreements.

Both the decisions and the regulation deal mainly with unilateral licences, which either stand by themselves or are part of a licensing network. This means that a relatively high proportion of EEC competition procedures in the field of patent licensing has dealt with unilateral licences.

A few publications in the Annual Reports are concerned with reciprocal licences and patent pools.

In respect of pure know-how licences we know two formal decisions and a few informal settlements. The Commission published recently a draft of a regulation exempting know-how licensing agreements.[9] It follows the model of the block exemption for patent licensing agreements.

Apart from the cases referred to above, licences have frequently been reviewed within the context of more complex agreements, dealing with subjects like joint research and development and specialization. These decisions fall outside the scope of the present contribution.

B. Competition within the licensed technology

The main concern of EEC competition policy has been to achieve a proper degree of competition within the licensed technology.

In broad outlines, the Commission's approach may be systematized as follows:

– demarcation of the boundaries within which certain restrictions can be allowed;

---

[8] Because of its importance for this subject, I include Commission decision Maize seed, OJ 12 October 1978 No. L. 286/23, and judgment of the Court of Justice in Case 257/78 Nungesser, 8 May 1982, ECR 1982, page 2015, which dealt with breeder's rights.
[9] OJ 12 August 1987, No. C. 214/2.

– determination of the competitive parameters which must remain unrestricted; and
– allowing some comparative reserved areas within the licensed technology.

Thus, the Commission has, in the first place, constituted itself the vigilant guardian of the free access to whatever is in the public domain, or might come into the public domain, due to expiration or annulment of the patent or to the fact that the know-how has become publicly known. This action has entailed the prohibition of no-challenge clauses,[10] because a successful challenging of the validity of a patent or of the secrecy of the licensed know-how may increase the public domain. It has lead to the prohibition of anything that reeks of restrictions outside the scope of an existing patent, like restrictions on, or royalties for, manufacture or sale without the use of a valid patent or secret know-how, or in parts of the common market where the patent has never been in force or is no more in force.[11]

In the second place, the Commission has made it clear that, even within the licensed technology, it does not admit restrictions on prices[12] or quantities.[13] These classic antitrust violations are also taboo in the area of competition that would not have existed without the licensing agreement.

In the third place, the Commission has created a system which allows the parties, operating within the licensed technology, to keep proper distances from one another. Its development has constituted the most elaborate part of the EEC action in the field of patent licensing. The definition of these relative reserved areas has mainly focused on territorial limits and their permeability: Exclusivity may be granted for a territory of any size,[14] but penetration into this territory should be free for resellers (the so-called 'parallel imports')[15] and not completely, or not for too long a time, impossible for other licensees)their so-called 'passive sales').[16] This delicate system is a result of three lines of reasoning:

---

[10] Article 1(3) of Decision AOIP/Beyrard, OJ 13 January 1976 No. L 6/8; Article 1(1) of Decision Vaessen/Moris, OJ 26 January 1979, No. L. 19/32; Article 3(1) of Regulation 2349/84; Case 193/83 Windsurfing International, 25 February 1986, ECR 1986, p. 611, recital 92; Article 3(4) of the Draft regulation on know-how licensing agreements.

[11] Article 1(4)(b) and (6) of Decision AOIP/Beyrard, OJ 13 January 1976, No. L 6/8; Article 3(4) of Regulation 2349/84; Case 193/83 Windsurfing International, 25 February 1986, ECR 1986, p. 611, recital 85; Article 3(5) of the Draft regulation on know-how licensing agreements.

[12] Article 3(6) of Regulation 2349/84; Article 3(8) of the Draft regulation on know-how licensing agreements.

[13] Article 3(5) of Regulation 2349/84; Article 3(7) of the Draft regulation on know-how licensing agreements.

[14] Article 1(1) of Regulation 2349/84; Decision Boussois/Interpane, OJ 19 February 1987 No. L 50/30; Article 1(1) of the Draft regulation on know-how licensig agreements.

[15] Article 3(11) of Regulation 2349/84; Article 3(12) of the Draft regulaton on know-how licensing agreements.

[16] Article 1(1)(6) and Article 3(10) of Regulation 2349/84; Article 1(1)(6) and 3(11) of the Draft regulation on know-how licensing agreements.

(1) territorial exclusivity is not always caught by Article 85 (1);[17]
(2) when it is, it may be necessary as an incentive for granting licences and for investing in exploiting a new technology;[18]
(3) absolute market isolation is unacceptable.[19]

Keeping distance may also be imposed in respect of technical fields of application;[20] but not in respect of product differentiation[21] and not in respect of customers.[22]

It should be noted that the Commission, in one of its drafts for Regulation 2349/84, intended to distinguish between larger and smaller undertakings: the possibility of preventing a licensee or licensor from selling directly into an exclusive territory would not be available to firms with a total annual turnover in excess of 100 million units of account.[23] The final regulation, however, does not make any distinction in respect of the importance of the parties.

C. Innovative competition

A firm's market success may depend on its having secured an advantage in the form of a new or better technology or product. Innovative competition has been recognized by the Commission as being protected by Article 85(1) EEC.[24]

Licensing is a way of marketing its direct result, the very source of the advantage over competitors. The reward for the innovator may be a lump-sum or a share in the financial return obtained by his contracting partner. Neither the abandonment by a licensor of his advantage over a competitor nor his acquisition of a financial share in the marketing of its results by the licensee have ever been viewed as a restriction of competition within the meaning of Article 85(1).

---

[17] Case 258/78 Nungesser, 8 May 1982, ECR 1982, page 2015, at 2069; rectial 11 of the preamble of Regulation 2349/84; recital 9 of the Draft regulation on know-how licensing agreements.
[18] Recital 12 of the preamble of Regulation 2349/84; recital 10 of the Draft regulation on know-how licensing agreements.
[19] Case 255/78 Nungesser, 8 May 1982, ECR 1982, page 2015, at 2070.
[20] Article 2(1)(3) of Regulation 2349/84; Article 2(1)(10) of the Draft regulation on know-how licensing.
[21] Case 193/83 Windsurfing International, 25 February 1986, not yet reported, recital 49.
[22] Article 3(7) of Regulation 2349/84; Article 3(6) of the Draft regulation on know-how licensing agreements.
[23] Proposal for a Commission Regulation on the application of Article 85(3) to certain categories of patent licensing agreements, OJ 3 March 1979 No. C. 58/11.
[24] Decision Beecham/Parker Davis, OJ 21 March 1979, No. L 70/15, § 25; Announcement Henkel-Colgate, Eighth Competition Report (1978), § 90. *See also: Fifteenth Competition Report*, pages 11–12.

Restrictions on the freedom of the parties in the field of research and development are, however, a matter of concern.[25] Pursuant to Article 3(3) of Regulation 2349/84 the block exemption is not available where one party is restricted from competing with the other party, with undertakings connected with the other party or with other undertakings within the common market in respect of research and development. On the other hand, there is no objection against an agreement between licensor and licensee for a mutual exchange and licensing of the results of individual research and development,[26] so that the parties may prevent one another from getting a new advantage over their partner.

Once, in 1981, the Commission had objected against the fact that two manufacturers made all their patents relating to a certain manufacturing process available to each other, because this exchange eliminated competition between the parties as regards technical innovation.[27] But in 1984 it declared that its block exemption also applies to reciprocal patent licences,[28] so that generally speaking restriction of innovative competition may be the consideration for the decision to license.

In the 1981 case referred to above,[29] Concast and Mannesmann remained autonomous as regards the exploitation of the results of the pooled technology. Nevertheless, the Commission mentioned a second restriction of competition resulting from their agreement: 'by concentrating a substantial package of know-how in their hands, it encouraged purchasers of continuous casting plant to deal with these two firms rather than competing third firms'. The Commission added that, between 1975 and 1977, the sales of the two firms accounted in total for some 60% of the market.

The Concast/Mannesmann case has been published under the heading 'Patent pools'. That term can, indeed, be applied to every situation in which patents of different origin are brought together in order to facilitate the exploitation of what is covered by their combined scope. However, Article 5 of Regulation No. 2349/84 creates different regimes for 'agreements between members of a patent pool which relate to the pooled patents' on the one hand and for 'reciprocal licences' on the other hand. Except for the case of territorial restrictions within the common market, the latter category enjoys the benefit of the block exemption, while the former category has been generally excluded from this favorable treatment.

This different treatment makes it necessary to determine the dividing line between the two categories. The Regulation is silent in this respect. My personal impression is that the exclusion of its Article 5(1)(1) concerns

---

[25] *See also* Regulation 418/85, recital 2.
[26] Notice of 24 December 1962, § I (D); Art. 2(10) of Regulation 2349/84.
[27] Concast/Mannesmann, *Eleventh Competition Report* (1982) §93.
[28] Art. 5(2) of Regulation 2349/84.
[29] Concast/Mannesmann, *Eleventh Competition Report* (1982), §93.

arrangements which make provision for the grant of licenses or sub-licenses under the combined patents to third parties.

Concast/Mannesmann is probably not such a situation. A review of the Commission's activity reveals the publication of only two interventions concerning patent pools as defined above. Both dealt with IGR Stereo Television.[30] The first one reveals that the joint acquisition by a group of undertakings of patents essential for operation on a certain market was not considered to be objectionable, but that such a pool is obliged to grant licenses to third parties. The second one declares that 'IGR and its members had secured a position which allowed them, through continued levying of royalties, to impose a sort of private import tax on the other European manufacturers of stereo television sets, particularly on the German market'. The case was closed when IGR agreed to lower considerably the royalty-rates for its European licensees, so that the observer still lacks detailed information.

One may wonder whether the Commission did not meet other patent pools. But it is certainly to be regretted that, when it deemed it necessary to intervene, it apparently shrank back from adopting formal decisions, which is the traditional means of acquiring experience and developing a policy. Instead, the observer must content himself with anodine announcements as quoted above.

4. Conclusions

EEC competition policy in respect of licensing of technology has not questioned the assumption that licensing should be promoted and has mainly focused on the effects on competition between the users of the licensed technology. The criteria for judging these effects have remained very abstract. A proposal to introduce a relevant factor like the importance of the contracting parties, or of either of them, as a criterion has been dropped.

Increased interest in possible competition between different technologies might lead to the amendment of a few accepted rules concerning clauses that are usually contained in licensing agreements. There may, e.g., be a reason to examine the significance in a particular case of an obligaton to disclose and license future individual developments of the technology.

But what seems to be more important, a more critical approach might lead to questioning the lawfulness of the agreement to grant and accept a licence itself. The issue would then be whether the advantage of this cooperation outweights its possible negative effects on innovative competition. This makes it necessary to pay more attention to the technology concerned and to the strength of the contracting parties and outsiders in particular in respect of that technology.

---

[30] *Eleventh Competition Report* (1982), §94; *Fourteenth Competition Report* (1985), §92.

The present development of EEC competition policy has rendered rather difficult an approach as advocated in the previous paragraph. This is not only due to the general tendency to abstraction, noted above. It also comes from the fact that it may require the explicit withdrawal in a particular case of the benefit of block exemptions pursuant to Regulation 2349/84 on patent licensing agreements and to a similar one on know-how agreements.

IX.   The European natural gas market

R.D. Visser

1.   Introduction

The discovery of a large deposit of gas on Dutch soil at Slochteren in 1959 was primarily viewed in the Netherlands as a matter of national economic importance. It was not thought at that time that the discovery would fundamentally change the energy scene in the whole of Western Europe. However, the discovery of the Groningen gas field at Slochteren was of great European significance. This reservoir proved to contain enormous quantities of natural gas. That initiated intensive exploratory activity in the North Sea which led to numerous further finds, not just in the Dutch sector of the continental shelf but also in the British and Norwegian sectors, which are at present of great importance for the European energy supply. One could say that the Groningen gas field has rendered possible the creation of a European gas market and the Netherlands occupies a key position between the large producing areas of the North Sea and the outlets on the West European mainland. The evolution of Dutch gas policy, which was initially national-oriented but which later took on an international character, is the subject of this study. This evolution has greatly contributed to the formation of a European gas market (the only remaining major non-participant is the United Kingdom). This European gas market will be an important factor in the primary energy supply of the European Community well into the next century.

2.   The beginning: the Sixties

The first political decision process regarding the sale of Groningen natural gas resulted in a memorandum on natural gas dated 11th July, 1962 from the then Minister of Economic Affairs, Mr J.W. de Pous, to the Lower Chamber of Parliament.[1] This memorandum outlined the sales and pricing policy to be pursued based on the principle of extracting from the available natural

---

[1] Kamerstukken II 1961/62, nr. 6767. *See also:* Handelingen II 1962/63 pp. 3007–3044, 1963/64 pp. 519–583, 1964/65 pp. 675–722. Further information is to be found in the Explanatory Memorandum to the annual draft Budgets of the Ministry of Economic Affairs.

gas (then estimated at a proven reserve of 150×10^9 m^3 and a possible reserve of 400×10^9 m^3) a maximum national economic advantage. In order to achieve this, rapid and full penetration of those sectors of the Dutch internal market which allowed the highest value of the gas to be realized was required, namely domestic use, space heating and high-grade industrial applications. This gas was to be supplied at prices which were sufficiently competitive compared with the prices of coal and oil products for the applications concerned to achieve a smooth transition to gas. In addition, a certain volume of gas (25×10^9 m^3) was to be made available at attractive prices and conditions for the promotion of industrial development projects. Even though the export of natural gas was not highlighted, the memorandum, however, stated that in order to serve national economic interests in the best way, the Government would monitor the destination of the natural gas, and thus be able to determine the quantities available for export; it was further stated that, for internal sales as well as for export, prices and terms of delivery were to be subject to Government approval.

In 1962, there were valid reasons for the Dutch Government to base its natural gas policy mainly on considerations of national politics.[2] In the early years of the EEC, there was no question yet of a common energy market, let alone a common energy policy. Admittedly, in June 1962 the executive bodies of the three Communities jointly submitted to the ECSC Council of Ministers a memorandum regarding a common energy policy, which contained the first proposals for arriving at a European energy market, but this could not really be given much chance of succeeding.[3] All the member states pursued energy policies which were determined by national considerations, and the main potential export destinations for Dutch natural gas, namely West Germany, Belgium and France, faced particularly grave problems concerning their voluminous internal coal production. As a matter of fact, owing to the labour-intensive nature of coal extraction in the Community making labour costs by far the greatest factor in total production costs, and owing further to the sharp increase in general wage levels in those years, the European coal industry was progressively less able to withstand the competition from coal imported from countries such as the United States where extraction was less labour-intensive and production costs were accordingly lower; moreover, there was a marked decrease worldwide in the costs of marine transport at that time. More important, however, was the growth of the oil industry. In the Sixties, the oil industry experienced an unprecedented growth and Western Europe saw the construction of large refineries, the laying of transnational pipelines and the development of

---

[2] Dr A.A. de Boer, *Aardgas en energiepolitiek*, ESB 1963, pp. 1080–1083.
[3] EEC Commission, 6th *General Report on the activities of the Community*, June 1963, pp. 147–155. *See also:* R. Wagenführ, EGKS 1952–1962, pp. 505–538, Luxemburg, 1963, and Supplement to *EC Bulletin* nr. 7–1966.

extensive distribution networks. In the oil industry labour, extraction and transport cost were comparatively low and production of oil was able to meet the rapid increase in demand. In 1960, coal still accounted for 54% of primary energy consumption in the Community; by 1962 this figure had dropped to 48%. In 1969, it was to be no more than 23%, while in that same year oil accounted for 62% of primary energy supply.[4] This decrease in the share of coal occurred despite vigorous measures taken by the coal producing countries, both in the form of direct subsidies and in the form of high taxes on oil consumption. In the Netherlands, it was anticipated as early as 1963 that, as a consequence of these developments, coal extraction in Limburg might have to be reduced. Two years later, a definite decision was taken to proceed with complete closure of all the mines, which in view of the natural gas profits to come would not need to create unsurmountable problems for the region in question.[5] Dutch energy policy was to be based on oil, with the rapidly-expanding refining and petrochemical activities in the Rhine Delta area, and on indigenous natural gas.

Within the scope of this policy, the export of natural gas was initially of secondary importance. The prime task of N.V. Nederlandse Gasunie, founded in 1963, was to promote domestic sales. An extensive pipeline transport network had to be constructed and all existing gas appliances had to be converted. Exploratory discussions began with gas companies in Belgium and West Germany, but these potential buyers adopted a wait-and-see attitude as they wanted to know at which level prices would be set for the Dutch domestic market. Prices depended ultimately on the Government and, therefore, the issue became emphatically political. Both the Lower Chamber of Parliament and organized interest groups urged that for social and economic reasons prices should be as low as possible, for public gas supply as well as for delivery to industrial customers.[6] The Government finally accepted the viewpoint that maximum penetration of natural gas was desirable in all consumer sectors of the domestic market, and not just in those sectors where natural gas can be used in high-grade applications.[7] The quantity of natural gas available for export was determined by the difference between the volume which would prove to be recoverable on a technically sound basis, and estimated domestic sales. The Government was bound by domestic political considerations to insist that border prices for export were under no circumstances lower than prices paid by domestic large-scale industrial consumers.

[4] Figures derived from the pertinent EEC Commission's General Reports on the activities of the Community.
[5] Parliamentary Proceedings concerning the finalization of the Budget for the State mines in Limburg, 1963 and following years.
[6] Cf. footnote 1.
[7] Speech by the Minister of Economic Affairs, Dr J.E. Andriessen at the inauguration of the Gasadviescommissie, 1 April 1964.

In September 1964 domestic prices, approved by the Minister, were published and during 1965 the first export contracts with Germany and Belgium were concluded, in which the border price for gas for industrial use almost corresponded to the marginal tariff for domestic large-scale industrial consumers. Thus it was possible to foresee a situation in which industrial users in Germany and Belgium would have to pay a higher price compared to Dutch industrial consumers. That this might lead to difficulties with the EEC was not something that was taken very seriously by the Dutch Government, although in Belgium this price discrepancy immediately received a great deal of political attention. Senator V. Leemans, member of the European Parliament, was the first to raise this matter at Community level and asked the Belgian Government to submit a complaint to the European Commission.[8]

Mr Leemans' action was followed by two members of the German Bundestag, who were also members of the European Parliament, namely Messrs. Burgbacher and Apel, who put searching questions on the same topic both to the Federal Government and to the European Commission.[9] With growing political pressure, the Commission decided to initiate an investigation into the sales policy of the Dutch Government regarding the Dutch natural gas on whether there was any violation of Article 37, or of Article 86, of the EEC Treaty. On the basis of this investigation, which took a number of years, the Commission finally concluded that in this instance there was no question of a violation of Article 37, and that in respect of Article 86 even though there was indeed a dominant economic position, the Commission found no abuse of this dominant position.[10]

The factors which the Commission had been taking into account in considering whether there was a breach of Article 37 may be summarized as follows: The agreements connected with the production licence of the Groningen gas provided that all natural gas extracted in this concession was to be delivered exclusively to Gasunie, regardless of the destination of this gas.[11] In view of the monopoly position thus gained by Gasunie in the marketing of this gas, and considering the influence the Dutch Government had retained on that marketing, the possible applicability of Article 37 was indeed conceivable. But no such exclusive delivery obligation was incorporated in the regulations for holders of concessions granted after 1963, whether on the Dutch mainland or in the Dutch sector of the continental shelf. For all these concessions granted after Groningen, an obligation to

---

[8] Chambre des Représentants de Belgique, 4–XII (1966/67) nr. 2, pp. 20, 21.
[9] OJ 3101/66; 1021/67; C 81/4 of 26 June 1969 and C 54/2 of 29 May 1972 (answer to written question by Mr. Vredeling). *See also:* European Parliament, *Communications to Members of the Committee for Energy, Research and Atomic Questions,* PE 22.133 of 21 May 1969 and PE 2.987 of 7 October 1969.
[10] Document 22.945/IV/69, rev. 2/70, not published.
[11] *Nederlandse Staatscourant* 1963, nr. 126.

sell to Gasunie came into effect only if the concession-holders wished to sell the gas on the Dutch domestic market.[12] This change in Dutch Government policy was probably due to the political pressure pursued at Community level and the ensuing action taken by the European Commission. But the concession-holders themselves soon realized that their commercial possibilities had been considerably extended by the effect of the EEC Treaty. Petroland, a Dutch subsidiary of Société Nationale Elf-Aquitaine, sold the gas from its concession in Friesland to Gaz de France and then entered into an agreement with Gasunie, whereby Petroland supplied gas to Gasunie and Gasunie supplied corresponding quantities of Groningen gas to Gaz de France. A similar arrangement was made by the holders of the Bergen concession in the province of North Holland, including Gelsenberg A.G., regarding the gas sold by them to Germany.[13] Owing to these factors, the European Commission was not able to conclude that Gasunie was an enterprise to which Article 37 of the EEC Treaty was applicable.

The fact that this initially concerned only small quantities of natural gas was not so important. Of far greater significance was the expectation that on the Dutch continental shelf, in particular, substantial gas deposits would be discovered. In the same year (1965) in which the Netherlands promulgated the Continental Shelf Mining Act,[14] the first natural gas well was struck in the British sector of the North Sea off eastern England. Shortly after, other major gas reservoirs were discovered in the same part of the North Sea. Because of the connection assumed to exist between geological structures, interest among oil companies in the adjoining Dutch sector of the North Sea intensified, an interest which already existed owing to wells drilled in the western part of the Netherlands. In 1967, the first exploration licences were granted under the implementing order of the Continental Shelf Mining Act. For Gasunie this meant that within a short period of time, a situation might develop in which it would have to negotiate for the purchase of natural gas (unless extracted in Groningen) in direct competition with its own foreign buyers. Prices would no longer be determined by domestic factors, but by international market conditions. This became a reality when in 1970 a consortium led by the American company Placid Oil was the first to discover a substantial gas deposit in the Dutch sector of the North Sea. Gasunie could not reach agreement with Placid and Placid sold the gas to West Germany. However, the Dutch Government intervened and forbade this export. This action by the Dutch Government caused the European Commission to intervene in turn on the basis of Article 34 of the EEC Treaty. These political skirmishes finally led to a compromise being reached in 1973: Placid was permitted to supply 50% (well over 2×10^9 m^3 a year) to its

---

[12] KB of 27 January 67, art. III, 25, *Staatsblad*, 1967, nr. 24.
[13] *N.V. Nederlandse Gasunie Annual Report 1970*, p. 12.
[14] *Staatsblad* 1965, nr. 428.

German buyers and the remaining 50% was to go to Gasunie.[15] Unlike the two previous cases, the Placid gas would be supplied direct to Germany. This was an important step towards the formation of a European natural gas market.

The true significance of the direct supply of gas to Germany is truly felt when these developments are compared with those in the United Kingdom. Since 1965 and within a relatively short space of time, a large number of important gas and oil finds were made in the UK sector. However, British legislation demanded that all gas extracted should be landed on the British mainland.[16] This meant that the British market remained separated from the market on the European continent, meaning that price formulation and sales policy regarding British natural gas were wholly determined by domestic factors and circumstances; in fact this situation persists to the present day and constitutes a serious impediment to the integration of the British gas market into the market of the rest of the EEC.

The second point in the investigation pursued by the European Commission into the marketing policy regarding Dutch natural gas was on a possible violation of Article 86 of the EEC Treaty. The Commission was of the opinion that there was indeed an – albeit limited – dominant position, because although natural gas is part of the total energy market, natural gas consumers, especially in the sector of small-scale consumption, are less susceptible to the price fluctuations of the products competing with natural gas once they have been connected to a distribution network. However, unlike Burgbacher and Apel, the Commission concluded that it was not permissible to compare consumers within the Netherlands and corresponding consumers in the countries importing Dutch natural gas, since the respective circumstances in which these consumers found themselves were not comparable. Evidently, the Commission was bearing in mind the differences between the energy policies pursued by the Netherlands on the one hand and the importing countries, especially West Germany, on the other. Partly owing to the high taxation of oil products, the relevant price level was considerably higher in West Germany than in the Netherlands, while sales to power stations were almost entirely restricted to coal by law. In addition, owing to a considerably lower density of the distribution network in Germany than that in the Netherlands, which derived in part from the Dutch policy of aiming for maximum penetration of the domestic market, distribution costs of natural gas were also higher in Germany than in the Netherlands. The Commission was of the opinion that the prices paid by

---

[15] *Gasunie 1973 Annual Report*, p. 9. *See also:* Lubbers and Lemckert, The Influence of Natural Gas on the Dutch Economy, pp. 99, 100 in: *The Economy and Politics of the Netherlands since 1945*, Richard T. Griffiths, editor, The Hague, 1980.

[16] Continental Shelf Act of 1964. Presently, the so-called 'landing requirement' is incorporated in Model Clause 27 of The Petroleum Production Regulations, 1982. *See also:* Frank Frazer, Gas Prospects in Western Europe, London, 1981, pp. 150–152.

foreign companies for delivery at the Dutch border and the price at which Gasunie itself bought Groningen gas should indeed be compared with each other. The Commission found the difference between these prices to be in accordance with the costs of the transport of the gas from Groningen to the respective delivery points at the border plus a reasonable compensation for investments made for this transport. Thus the border prices were not considered unfair within the meaning of Article 86 of the EEC Treaty.

Here the Commission used an argument which it had already employed in its provisional answer to Brugbacher in 1966, namely that 'in a truly common market, and within the framework of an energy policy as pursued by the Commission, the prices at which gas is supplied to the end users may in principle differ only according to the mode of delivery and the distance between the consumer and the place of extraction'.[17] This argument, the principle of cost price, which was derived from pricing policies in accordance with the provisions of the ECSC Treaty, may have been understandable at the time, but it was nevertheless a precarious one, for it applies only in market situations where there is no interference in the course of free competition from external, non-market factors.

The alternative to the principle of cost price is the principle of market value. This means, in the present case, that the value of the natural gas produced is ultimately determined by the price the end users are prepared to pay in relation to the price of alternative energy sources available to them. In the sectors of household consumption and small-scale industrial consumption the alternative sources of energy are generally domestic heating oil and light fuel oil, respectively, while in the sector of large-scale industrial consumers and power stations the market value almost always corresponds to the price of heavy fuel oil or coal. The value of natural gas is highest in the first sector where consumption displays considerable fluctuations such as winter peaks and summer troughs. In the other sector, the value of natural gas is lowest, but offtake per individual consumer is large and arrangements for temporary interruption of supply can be made in many cases because the consumer has dual firing at his disposal and is able to switch to fuel oil in times of high gas consumption. Owing to the capital-intensive nature of the transport and distribution systems for natural gas it is economically essential for the load-factor of these systems to be maintained at a level which is both high and constant. Gas companies such as Gasunie – but the same holds true for Ruhrgas, Gaz de France and the Belgian Distrigaz – will have to strive for an optimum mix of high-grade and low-grade sales in their marketing areas in order to attain as high and constant a load-factor as possible. In practice, interruptible deliveries to large-scale industrial users do not always prove sufficiently capable of achieving this, thus creating a need for storage facilities at strategic locations in the marketing area – above ground in tanks

[17] Cf. footnote 9.

as in the Netherlands on the 'Maasvlakte' near Rotterdam, or below ground, for example in salt domes as in the countries surrounding us – which function as peak-shavers, thereby improving the efficiency of the distribution systems concerned and, in addition, enhancing the security of gas supply.[18] To state the matter in a nutshell and without considering its fiscal aspects: if the true market value of the natural gas is realized at the level of the end users in these different consumer sectors, and capital costs and the operational costs of the transportation, storage and distribution infrastructures are subtracted from the total proceeds, one obtains a net-back at the level of the gas companies which constitutes a break-even point, i.e. this net-back corresponds to the maximum buying price for the gas companies which allows them profitably to maintain their share of the energy market.

Whenever the gas companies are able to buy, for longer periods, substantial volumes of natural gas at prices below this break-even point, an increasing penetration of natural gas in the energy market ensues, primarily at the expense of competing oil products, but partly also at the expense of coal. This was the situation in the Sixties. It was mainly due to the fact that the Netherlands had chosen to aim for maximum penetration of the domestic natural gas market, which – because the border prices for foreign buyers had to stand in a reasonable relation to the buying price for Gasunie – also rendered possible a rapid penetration of export markets. Considering conditions in the energy market at the time and the enormous extent of Dutch gas reserves which had in the meantime been proven, this choice of a rapid penetration was indeed understandable. But in the next decade the OPEC countries were to introduce production restrictions for crude oil, causing the market value of the oil products competing with natural gas to multiply several times compared with their values in the Sixties. Thus a considerable discrepancy was to develop between the break-even point on the one hand and the current prices to be paid by the gas companies for Dutch gas on the other. If this discrepancy was not quickly eliminated, the demand for Dutch gas would grow to such an extent that Dutch production would not possibly be able to meet it.[19] In the same period, the countries to which Dutch natural gas was exported increasingly began to obtain natural gas from third countries (Norway, the Soviet Union, Algeria) at buying prices which were indeed geared to the break-even point, thus giving rise to the possibility that gas companies in those countries would use the cheaper Dutch gas to subsidize the cost of importing gas from such third countries. The difficulties involved in eliminating this discrepancy will be discussed in the next part of this study. Suffice it to say in this part that the principle of cost price did not retain its validity in the changed circumstances of the Seventies, while the

---

[18] *See*, for instance, Ruhrgas A.G. *1975 Annual Report*, pp. 21–25 and *Gasunie 1979 Annual Report*, pp. 9–12.

[19] Explanatory Memorandum to the 1972 draft Budget of the Minister of Economic Affairs.

principle of market value did. This holds true not only for natural gas, but for all sources of energy, including European coal. This created a problem concerning the energy policy to be adopted by the Community, which, from the Sixties onwards, had taken as its point of departure price systems based on the principle of cost price as laid down in the ECSC Treaty. Not until the Eighties was the Community able to reach political consensus on the principle of market value as the basis of an integrated energy policy.[20]

3. The Oil Crisis and the Seventies

In 1970, the reasonably stable energy prices of the Sixties suddenly came to an end. Expansion of economic growth produced a sharp increase in energy demand. Oil prices began to rise considerably. The post-1970 structural changes affecting the prices of oil and thus also the prices of the oil products competing with natural gas could not be reflected without considerable delay in the actual prices for natural gas by price systems for the sale of natural gas as they had developed in the preceding years, systems based on fixed prices which were renegotiable if conditions changed. Therefore, demand for natural gas was greatly stimulated. In 1970, exports of Dutch natural gas rose by nearly 50% compared with 1969 to 11.3×10^9 m^3, while domestic sales rose by well over 70% to over 20×10^9 m^3.[21] In 1971, these percentages were to be substantially higher still. Soon there was increasing support for the idea that the existing price system for export should be replaced by a system in which border prices were directly linked to the price fluctuations of the oil products competing with natural gas. Following the oil production restrictions instituted by the OPEC countries in 1973, this idea gained the upper hand.[22] Nevertheless, the transition to the new price system could only take place very gradually, because it depended ultimately to the extent to which this linkage to oil prices could be realized at the level of the end-consumers in the importing countries. At the end of 1974, a price system had been arranged by Gasunie with its foreign purchasers for 85% of the total export obligations, in which the border price was gradually to become linked to the price of heavy fuel oil. Despite considerable price increase resulting from the new price structure, exports increased by almost 300% to 50.6×10^9 m^3 from 1971 to 1976, which corresponded to well over half the total natural gas consumption of the countries importing Dutch natural gas. This result was possible because of the continuing demand for Dutch natural gas. However, no further increase in export volume was to occur after 1976. Between 1976 and 1980, export volume remained constant

---

[20] Council Recommendation No. 83/230/EEC of 21 April 1983, OJ L 123 of 11 May 1983.
[21] Figures derived from pertinent *Gasunie Annual Reports*.
[22] Kamerstukken II 1974/75, nr. 13122 (Energienota).

at about 50×10^9 m³. Then there was a sudden drop to a level of around 35 $\times 10^9$ m³ in 1982. At this export volume, the market share of Dutch natural gas in the export markets dropped to about 28%.[23] The reason for this sudden drop will be discussed in the third part of this study. Suffice it to say here that not until 1985 the situation was reached that border prices actually did follow the real market value of natural gas, because the price formula incorporated, in weighted averages, both the prices of low-sulphur fuel oil and of domestic heating oil as reference prices.

In the period 1974–1976, complete linkage to the price of heavy fuel oil was achieved in domestic sales to large-scale industrial consumers, where there had already been a limited linkage. But in the sectors of household consumption and other small-scale consumption, prices in 1976 were on average still 30% below the price of replacement fuel. For the time being, political resistance to the implementation of the principle of market value in these sectors was too strong:[24] not until 1983 would a political decision be taken to actually implement the principle of market value as the only and decisive criterion in the sale of natural gas in all sectors. But in the Energy Memorandum dated 26th September, 1974, from the then Minister of Economic Affairs, Mr R.F.M. Lubbers, a reappraisal of domestic sales policies was announced, in which an economically sound mix was to be achieved between sales in high-grade consumption sectors and those sectors in which natural gas utilization was not so low-grade that the use of other energy sources was to be preferred.[25] Among other things, the delivery of natural gas to power stations was to be gradually reduced. Thus the policy of maximum penetration of natural gas in the domestic market came to an end. In 1975, the share of natural gas in total primary energy consumption in the Netherlands still reached 55%, but after that year a gradual decrease set in. In 1980, its share was 44%. However, it did not at all mean that this policy reappraisal had been fully carried out. Even today this is not yet entirely the case.

Together with the introduction of the new price systems, the Dutch Government also took measures to increase its income from the sale of Groningen natural gas, which at the time still constituted by far the greatest part of total Dutch natural gas production. The 1974 Energy Memorandum announced a review of the 'additional proceeds arrangement' regarding Groningen gas, which would considerably increase the Government take from the proceeds of the gas. In this connection, it was also decided to set the future net profits of Gasunie at Dfl. 80 million a year from 1975 onwards. This last measure meant that, both for domestic sales and for export,

[23] Figures derived from pertinent *Gasunie Annual Reports*.
[24] De prijs van het aardgas, advies uitgebracht door de Algemene Energieraad aan de Minister van Economische Zaken op 28 juni 1983, Den Haag, 1983.
[25] Energienota referred to in footnote 22.

proceeds at the wellhead would in fact be directly determined by the price of the gas at the level of the end-consumers. In other words: proceeds at the wellhead would in the long term have to equal the net-back of the real market value of the natural gas extracted. With these measures, the Netherlands would align itself with Norway and other countries exporting natural gas to the European Community. This alignment with other gas-exporting countries slowly but surely produced reasonably similar conditions in the natural gas market in the continental countries of the Community. (Reasonably, since the differences in consumer tax for energy sources between the Member States precluded – and still do so – the development of a truly uniform market). In this process the Netherlands, by far the largest exporter of natural gas in the Western European natural gas market, was to play the most important part. The Dutch Government's national-oriented policy of the Sixties was to be replaced increasingly by an international-oriented policy. The importance of this policy change for the Community is clearly seen on comparing this development with the development in the United Kingdom, which in size was the second largest producer of natural gas in the Community. In the UK, the energy policy remained national-oriented, resulting in a continuing isolation of the UK from natural gas developments in the Continent.

The implementation of the principle of market value right back to the wellhead meant that Gasunie would now have to buy all their gas on the basis of net-backed market value. The privileged position which Gasunie had occupied within the European gas market owing to its exclusive right to Groningen gas came to an end. From a European point of view, this was equally important. As far as purchase was concerned, Gasunie would be on equal terms with its foreign customers such as Ruhrgas, Gaz de France and the Belgian company Distrigaz. Moreover, the 1974 Energy Memorandum made it clear that the speed with which the Groningen gas deposit was being depleted was to be slowed down considerably, while the purchase of gas elsewhere was to become a matter of greater priority.

With regard to export, the said Energy Memorandum further announced that no additional quantities of natural gas would be available beyond the volumes laid down in current contracts and that no new contracts would be entered into. This prompted foreign gas companies to urgently look out for supplementary volumes from elsewhere in order to be able to guarantee a continuing gas supply for the future in their respective marketing areas. To this must be added the expectation of a further increase in energy consumption in Western Europe, and the general feeling of uncertainty regarding developments connected with oil supply. All these factors caused the demand for natural gas from new sources to increase sharply, and prices to remain subject to a continuous upward pressure in the Seventies.

These market-generated interests for exploration and production of natural gas, particularly in the North Sea area, were soon successful. In 1975, the first gas was delivered from the Dutch continental shelf. By 1980, this was already to involve a quantity of about 23×10^9 mm^3, while proven reserves in the Dutch continental shelf in that year amounted to about 300×10^9 m^3 and possible reserves were estimated at 400×10^9 m^3. Total Dutch proven reserves in 1980 amounted to $1,570 \times 10^9$ m^3, while total possible reserves in that year were estimated at $2,320 \times 10^9$ m^3. In 1977, the Ekofisk field began production in the Norweigan sector of the North Sea. Gas reserves in the geological structures of this area were estimated at well over 250×10^9 m^3. In 1980, recoverable reserves in the entire Norwegian continental shelf were estimated at $1,700 \times 10^9$ m^3, with the expectation that it might contain much more gas.[26]

From the European point of view, the Ekofisk project is of great significance in several respects. It was the first project in the history of the oil industry to be undertaken so far offshore and in such deep waters (70 meters), and moreover it had to withstand severe weather conditions. New technologies were developed and tested here which would prove to be of great importance to oil and gas production in the deeper waters further north in the North Sea. Owing to the great financial, economical and technical risks connected with this project (it involved 'associated gas', i.e. natural gas surfacing during the production of oil and deliverable as natural gas only after separation, of which the whole reserve – whatever this would turn out to be – had to be taken off in quantities keeping step with oil production, and which had to be transported via a 438 km pipeline across the seabed) a consortium had been formed for the purchase of this gas with Gasunie, Ruhrgas, Gaz de France and Distrigaz as its principal members. Collaboration within a consortium between gas companies from different Member States was to become increasingly widespread after this, not only in connection with Norwegian gas but also, for example, with gas from the Soviet Union. Besides the necesssary spreading of risks, there was a further reason for the formation of consortia: the greater the distance across which the gas needs to be transported, the more inflexible does the load-factor become economically, which in the case of associated gas is already inflexible on technical grounds. However, a constant stream of gas has to be absorbed by a market in which consumption patterns, as explained before, are subject to great variations. Now, the larger the sales market, the more possibilities there are of obviating such variations through e.g. peak-shaving and underground storage and, therefore, of buying as economically as possible, that is to say, at a load-factor which is constant and as high as possible. The fact that the Community natural gas market was to an important extent already beginning to function as a large single market contributed greatly to the rapid availability, through these buying consortia, of large quantities of Norwegian and Soviet gas in the Community. In turn, the fact that these large quantities of gas which were delivered at a constant and high load-

[26] *Gasunie 1981 Annual Report* pp. 6–15. *See also:* Frazer, op. cit., pp. 47–55.

factor needed to be absorbed, greatly promoted the further development of the Community gas market. The European Commission was quick to recognize the significance of this for the Community and in its Communication of 2 June 1980 to the Council of Ministers concerning Community action in the natural gas supply sector, it proposed especially 'to encourage the co-operation between the governments of Member States and between gas undertakings for the realization of large importation projects for supplies from third parties'.[27]

At least equally important, in respect of the formation of a European gas market, was the construction of intra-Community pipeline systems to transport gas imported from third countries, in addition to the already developed infrastructure for the sale of Groningen gas in the Community. Norwegian gas has a higher calorific value than Groningen gas. It cannot simply be mixed with Groningen gas, because gas burners have only limited tolerance regarding calorific value. Mixing with Groningen gas and simultaneously lowering the resulting calorific value by adding air or nitrogen is technically and economically possible only on a limited scale. This meant that a separate system of main transport lines for high-calorie gas had to be constructed.[28] *Figure 1* shows the European grid of main transport lines (both for high-calorie gas and for gas of Groningen quality), as it has developed till now. Norwegian gas arrives at Emden. From there, a pipeline system runs to the Frankfurt region via the Ruhr area. High-calorie and Groningen gas are mixed in the Ruhr area for local sale. South of Frankfurt, only high-calorie gas is presently sold. A second main transport line runs directly from Emden to Dutch territory, where it is connected to the pipeline system completed in 1974, which initially was used only to transport high-calorie gas from the Annerveen field in Drenthe to Northern Italy. This system is presently used for the transport of both Annerveen gas and of high-calorie gas from the Dutch continental shelf and from Norway. Gasunie transports the gas to the border in South Limburg, at which point the system is split in two. Distrigaz and Gaz de France take up the quantities laid down in their respective purchase contracts and then transport this gas to their customers in Belgium and France via a pipeline system belonging to SA 'SEGEO' Société Européenne du Gazoduc Est-Ouest, a joint enterprise of Distrigaz and Gaz de France.[29] The remaining gas is transported through West Germany to Basle by the Trans Europa Naturgas Pipeline GmbH, an enterprise owned jointly by Ruhrgas A.G. and the Italian Company SNAM SpA.[30] From there, this pipeline crosses the Swiss Alps into Northern Italy.

---

[27] COM (80) 295 final of 2 June 1980.
[28] C. Brecht, The European Gas Grid, paper presented at the European Petroleum and Gas Conference Amsterdam, 1978.
[29] *Distrigaz S.A. Annual Reports.*
[30] *Ruhrgas A.G. Annual Reports.*

Since 1986, this pipline system has been connected to the TRANSMED pipeline system, built with support from the European Investment Bank and 2,900 km long, which transports Algerian gas from the deposits at Hassi-R'Mel to the Italian mainland via the Mediterranean, Sicily and the Strait of Messina.[31] Thus an integrated main transport system has been realized, which is fed by Norwegian and Dutch natural gas on the one hand and by gas from Algeria on the other, which possesses proven reserves of at least $3,000 \times 10^9$ m^3. In the course of the Eighties, Norwegian supply to this system was to be substantially expanded by the connection of the gas production from newly-discovered Norwegian offshore deposits between 59° and 62° North (including the Heimdal, Gullfaks and Statfjord fields) to a collecting station for these gas streams built at the beginning of the Ekofisk pipeline connection to Emden, the 'Ekofisk-Centre'.

Besides this North-South system, an equally important East-West system of main transport lines has developed in Europe since the Seventies. By about 1970, Austria was already receiving Soviet natural gas from fields in the European part of the Soviet Union. The first purchase contracts concluded by Ruhrgas and the Italian gas company SNAM with the Soviet Union date from the same time. In 1974 – the same year in which the pipeline from the Annerveen field to Italy was completed – the first Soviet natural gas was supplied to Northern Italy via Austria through a pipeline which is connected to the Soviet pipeline system in Czechoslovakia. Both pipelines link up near Milan. In 1973, Ruhrgas, Gaz de France and the Austrian OMV AG formed a consortium for the purchase of substantial quantities of natural gas from the Soviet Union, and also from Iran. After the purchase contracts had been agreed in 1975, Ruhrgas and Gaz de France founded a joint venture in 1976, MEGAL G.m.b.H. Mittel-Europäische Gasleitungsgesellschaft, for the transport from the Czech-German border to the German-French border of gas from the Soviet Union and Iran. A second connection of the MEGAL system to the Soviet pipeline system was to be established via Austria. Owing to the political upheaval in Iran in 1979, deliveries from that country did not take place in the end, so that the MEGAL system was used only for the transport of Soviet gas. In 1981, new agreements were reached, whereby natural gas from North-west Siberia was to be delivered to West Germany, France, Italy, Austria and Switzerland via a pipeline system of 5,500 km.[32] (Initially, Gasunie and Distrigaz were also part of the purchase consortium, but they finally withdrew.) Thus Western Europe gained access to gas deposits with recoverable reserves of at least $16,000 \times 10^9$ m^3. When these deliveries, which began in 1984, will reach their plateau level in 1992, West Germany will take off some 10.5 to 13 $\times$ 10^9 m^3 a year and France 6 to 8 $\times 10^9$ m^3 a year via the MEGAL-system. In

---

[31] *SNAM S.p.A. Annual Reports* as from 1979 onwards.
[32] *Ruhrgas A.G. Annual Reports.*

France, MEGAL via main transport lines of Gaz de France is connected to terminals at Fos (near Marseilles), Montoir de Bretagne (near Saint Nazaire) and Le Havre, where liquefied natural gas (LNG) is landed from Algeria, while another main transport line runs to Belgium and is connected to the terminal for the supply of LNG from Algeria, which was completed at Zeebrugge in 1987. In 1985, France and Belgium together received well over 9×10^9 m^3 natural gas in the form of LNG from Algeria. In the same year, Italy received 6.8×10^9 m^3 Algerian gas via the TRANSMED pipeline. As is the case with the North-South system, this system is also fed from two sides. Because both systems are also connected to one another, they constitute an infrastructure of intra-Community pipeline systems which is of great importance for ensuring natural gas supply in the continental part of the Community.[33]

4. The Present Decade and the Future

The application of the real market value as the basis of pricing for natural gas at the level of end-consumers, and the use of the net-back of this market value as the basis of pricing for natural gas at the wellhead, led to the formation of a reasonably coherent natural gas market; thus the possibilities were created for the gas companies in the different Member States to purchase natural gas jointly in consortia from third countries; and the co-operation between these gas companies in the realization of an intra-Community network of main transport lines – these are in fact the main cornerstones of the present European gas market.

Since the beginning of the Eighties, these cornerstones have received a great deal of attention from the European Commission. This attention was triggered primarily by the conflict that developed between the United States and its Western European allies in 1980 regarding deliveries of construction materials to the Soviet Union for the building of the pipeline which was to transport Siberian natural gas to Western Europe. This also involved the question of whether Soviet natural gas would be a reliable factor in the long-term safety of Western European gas supply, and whether Western Europe was not making itself too dependent on the Soviet Union in this respect. Secondly, this attention was due to the fact that Algeria, also in 1980, temporarily suspended its deliveries of LNG to Gaz de France, because the latter was not willing to accept a price review desired by Algeria entailing that FOB prices would have to be paid which, on the basis of calorific value, were equal to the FOB prices for Algerian crude oil, and would thus result in a sharp increase in price. At the same time, Libya

[33] Frazer, op. cit. pp. 44, 45, 61–67 and 204–208. A. Giraud and X. Boy de la Tour, Géopolitique du Pétrole et du Gaz, Paris, 1987, pp. 381–389.

(again temporarily) suspended its LNG deliveries to Italy for the same reason.

Both events caused concern to the Commission about the short-term as well as the long-term security of natural gas supply.[34] Regarding the short term, the Commission, in collaboration with experts from the Member States, carried out various investigations during the period 1982–1986 into the extent that the effects of a sudden interruption of a major supply stream of natural gas from third countries might be absorbed. These studies especially emphasized the significance of the intra-Community network of main transport lines, and of the co-operation of the gas companies in the functioning of this network, in absorbing sudden stagnations in natural gas supply. From this the Commission concluded that further expansion of the intra-Community network and the continuing co-operation of the gas companies in this matter needed to be encouraged.[35] A second factor was the rapid and flexible availability of the natural gas present within the Community. The investigation by the Commission showed that, taking into account measures executed and planned in 1986 with regard to the underground storage of natural gas and interruptible deliveries to large consumers, taking further into account the proven flexibility in the production of natural gas from fields within the Community, natural gas supply in those Member States that were linked to one another through the intra-Community network could, in the period to 1990, be considered as being guaranteed for at least nine months in the case of a supply interruption from third countries up to an amount equal to 25% of total supplies from third countries.[36] In this respect, developments relating to Dutch natural gas are also significant, although the Commission does not specifically mention this. Production restrictions implemented for the Groningen gas field since the second half of the Seventies (whereas newly-found natural gas deposits were immediately brought into full production) have had as a result that of the total Dutch natural gas production for 1986, onshore and offshore, which amounted to 73×10^9 m^3, only 40×10^9 m^3 derived from the Groningen field. In 1976, the year of its highest production, the Groningen field supplied 83×10^9 m^3. Because pressure in the reservoir has not yet significantly decreased, it may be concluded that the Groningen field had a reserve production capacity of

[34] COM (80) 731 final of 21 November 1980,
COM (81) 530 final of 27 October 1981,
COM (82) 45 final of 16 March 1982,
COM (82) 653 final of 15 October 1982,
COM (84) 120 final of 13 April 1984, and
COM (84) 583 final of 26 October 1984.
See also: European Parliament, Working Documents 1983–1984, Document 1-1512/83 of 12 March 1984: Report on European Community Gas Policy, Rapporteur Mr Allan Rogers.
[35] COM (86) 518 final, p. 4.
[36] Idem, p. 3.

some 40×10^9 m^3 per annum in 1986.[37] According to the most recent planning at Gasunie, in 1990 only 23×10^9 m^3 of a total Dutch production of 63×10^9 m^3 will come from the Groningen gas field.[38] Thus the reserve production capacity of the Groningen field will certainly be maintained in the coming years. This 'buffer', which has in fact already been used for the benefit of Italy at the end of 1980 when Libya suddenly suspended delivery of LNG, is of vital importance to the Community not only in case there should again be interruptions in gas delivery from third countries, but also, more generally, for absorbing market fluctuations (for example during severe winters), for which purpose the gas delivery systems from third countries importing into the Community are too inflexible. In this respect, Groningen gas still occupies a key position for the European gas supply. Because reservoir pressure will be decreasing substantially in the Groningen gas field in the Nineties, it is already necessary to make adequate technical provisions in order to be able to guarantee this 'buffer' function for the long-term future.

Regarding the security of a long-term natural gas supply, the Commission on the one hand continued a number of policies developed in the Seventies, such as encouraging high-grade application of natural gas, stimulating exploration and production of natural gas deposits within the Community and the diversification of the import of natural gas to encompass as many third countries as possible. On the other hand, however, in its planning document 'Energy 2000', which appeared in 1985, the Commission did in fact formulate new policy projections, primarily in reaction to the drastic increase in oil prices of 1979 and the concomitant economic recession. These new policy projections were aimed at the possibility of restructuring Community energy supply, involving, in particular, a reduction of the share of oil in primary energy supply that would make the European economy less susceptible to the price fluctuations of oil. With regard to natural gas, the Commission did accept that the real market value currently was determined by a weighted average for the prices of domestic heating oil and light and heavy fuel oil, but it would not exclude the possibility that this price structure might be discarded in the future, thus making possible gas prices below parity with the relevant oil products.[39] In this case, the price of natural gas would in part be determined by the prices of coal, and natural gas could again be used to a greater extent for low-grade applications. According to this projection, in the year 2000 the share of natural gas in the Community's primary energy supply would amount to 20%, while according to the projection maintaining the price of natural gas at parity with oil products, this share

---

[37] Figures derived from pertinent *Gasunie Annual Reports*.
[38] Gasunie 1987 Gas Marketing Plan.
[39] Energy 2000, SEC (85) 324 final, pp. 7 and 37–39.

would be 17%. (Both projections were based on a crude oil price which, expressed in 1983 dollars, would have risen to $35 per barrel).

The sudden drop in oil prices, which occurred in 1986 as a result of the abandonment of the production level agreed within OPEC, again caused uncertainty about future developments concerning the Community's long-term energy supply. At the end of 1986, the European Commission expressed its concern about the possibility that the share of coal in primary energy supply might again drop, after having remained comparatively stable since 1969, and thus increase the Community's dependence on imported oil. On the basis of these considerations, the Commission was of the opinion that, as far as natural gas was concerned, a share of 18% of the Community's primary energy supply should be regarded as an absolute minimum: 'An increased share beyond the current 18% (EUR 12) might mitigate any tendency to increased dependence on oil imports due to low oil prices'.[40] The Commission reiterated its view that in order to realize a greater share for natural gas, gas prices indeed had to be decoupled from oil prices.

The Commission's view requires further discussion. Firstly, a gradual descent of the gas price to below oil parity wil not lead to a proportional increase in consumption. Only after the gas price has dropped firmly to below a specific level will a new category of consumers manifest itself, belonging mainly to the sector of large-scale consumption. This means that at a certain juncture in the price decline, demand will suddenly increase very sharply. In this connection, the figures used by the Commission seem somewhat peculiar. In the Commission's projection, an increase by 3% (i.e. from 17% to 20%) in the share of natural gas in primary energy consumption would amount to an expansion from 225×10^9 m^3 to 232×10^9 m^3 in 2000, which corresponds to about 6 million tons of oil. In this case, the share of oil would decrease by 1.4% from 439 million tons to 433 million tons in 2000.[41] These are very marginal changes indeed. However, as soon as a substantial decrease in the price of gas below parity with competing oil products prompts a new category of buyers to enter the market, it must rather be expected that demand will increase not just by 7×10^9 m^3, but – considering the experience of the Sixties – by a multiple of that in a single leap. An increase of at least $50-70 \times 10^9$ m^3 would seem to be a more likely assumption, which would probably knock the bottom out of the market. But how would the supply side of the market react to this at the international level?

Is it realistic, in an international context, to suppose that the Community, as an importer of natural gas, would unilaterally be able to achieve a structural break with oil parity? This question is certainly relevant to the safeguarding of the Community's long-term energy supply. The following

---

[40] COM (86) 518 final, pp. 8, 9.
[41] Figures derived from Energy 2000, p. 14.

might be noted in this respect. Investment costs of the supply systems for natural gas from third countries to the Community, as well as costs of the infrastructure for transport, storage and distribution thereof within the Community, are substantially higher than the corresponding costs of the transport and refining of crude oil and infrastructure for the transport, storage and distribution of oil products. On the basis of parity between the prices of natural gas and competing oil products at the level of the end-consumers in the Community, this means that the net-back at wellhead for natural gas will always be lower than that for oil.[42] Now, if the price of natural gas were to drop below that parity, which would be necessary in order to substantially increase the share of natural gas in primary energy supply compared with that of oil, the relative net-back for natural gas would deteriorate further. However, it is open to question whether the countries that possess natural gas reserves which might meet the Community's future demand would be willing to accept such a disadvantageous net-back ratio. These reserves lie mainly in countries (Norway, the Soviet Union, the Middle East, Algeria, Nigeria) which are also important oil producers, and which together own by far the greatest proportion of world oil reserves. It does not seem very likely that these countries would want to accept the development of such a kind of gas-to-oil competition from which, with regard to their revenue, they would emerge as losers.[43]

It may further be observed in this connection that the 1980 price dispute between Gaz de France and the Algerian state enterprise Sonatrach is not to be regarded as a passing incident, but rather as a forerunner of future developments. In June 1980, the OPEC states reacted with a statement in which they 'reiterated their determination to set gas prices in line with those of crude oil in order to achieve a coherent marketing policy for their hydrocarbons'.[44] (This parity based on calorific value means that the market value of the light fractions of oil used for automotive purposes, a value which is higher than that of middle distillates, is brought to bear on the price of natural gas although natural gas is not in competition with those light fractions.) The renegotiations between Gaz de France and Sonatrach ultimately led to a new base price being agreed on in 1982, which was linked to a basket of a number of crude oil prices. In 1981, the Belgian company Distrigaz had already accepted a similar price formula for its LNG offtakes from Sonatrach. Thus these prices are higher than the prices presently charged by the Soviet Union and Norway for their natural gas deliveries to the Community, but due allowance has to be made for the fact that Algerian

---

[42] *Natural Gas Prospects to 2000*, study by the Secretariat of the International Energy Agency, Paris, 1982, Chapter 7.
[43] Proved natural gas reserves at end 1985 were for USSR 43% and for OPEC countries 32% of proved world natural gas reserves. Western Europe (incl. UK) had 6.5% (*BP Statistical Review of World Energy*, 1986).
[44] Cited at p. 139 of the study referred to in footnote 42.

supplies to France and Belgium are in the form of LNG, and that investment costs for liquefication and regasification are substantial, so that net-
back at wellhead is lower than in all current cases in which natural gas is
supplied to the Community by pipeline. It seems likely that in the long term,
the transport of natural gas to the Community will increasingly have to take
place in the form of LNG rather than via pipelines, because the gas will
have to come from increasingly remote locations and because pipeline trans-
mission has inherent economic limits. Regarding its conclusions on long-
term Community energy supply, the European Commission could indeed be
criticized for having given too much emphasis to what might be called
'consumers' logic' at the expense of what might be termed 'producers' logic.'
For this reason, its portrayal of the actual conditions in the international
energy market is somewhat unbalanced. It is hardly possible to base a
projection for the Community's energy policy on the relative market shares
of the different energy sources as consumers would like to see them, because
these market shares are the uncertain outcome of an extremely complicated
interplay of the forces of supply and demand, in which long-term price
expectations on both sides of this market are ultimately the decisive factor.

Until the end of the Seventies, expectations, for the development of
prices and for the growth of European energy consumption to the end of the
century were roughly parallel on both sides of the international gas market.
These expectations were favourable and Community imports of natural gas,
it seemed, could without much difficulty be brought to a level at which gas
supply seemed adequately guaranteed to the year 2000 and even beyond.
Nevertheless, as a result of the economic recession which ensued when the
oil price more than doubled in 1979, 1980 unexpectedly saw a considerable
drop in natural gas consumption and in energy consumption in general in
Europe. There was a possibility of a substantial surplus supply of natural gas
developing, but in spite hereof price parity between natural gas and competing oil products remained in full force in the Community natural gas
market. To an important if not decisive extent this was due to the fact that
the Netherlands, still the major natural gas supplier of the Community,
unabatedly clung on to this parity. Mention may be made here of the
appointment in 1980 of a Government Commissioner for natural gas export
prices, Mr D.P. Spierenburg, who was charged to bring about an adjustment
of the price of natural gas in line with its value by negotiating on behalf of
the Dutch Government with foreign purchasers and the governments involved – but with the big stick of the Natural Gas Prices Law of 1974 in
hand if negotiation failed.[45] The Dutch Government was particularly concerned to achieve a structural solution, so that a discrepancy between the
natural gas price and the oil price would no longer be possible in the future.
This pricing policy was, however, achieved at the cost of a considerable

---

[45] *Nederlandse Staatscourant* 1980, nr. 111.

136

diminution of the share of Dutch natural gas in the export markets, mainly, as has been noted above, in the sector of low-grade applications. But even now that the market had changed, Dutch policy consistently followed 'producers' logic': in the long term, maintaining price is more important than maintaining market share.

This 'producers' logic' underlies the review of Dutch natural gas policy as set out in September 1983 in the Explanatory Memorandum to the draft Budget for his Department by the then Minister of Economic Affairs, Mr G.M.V. van Aardenne.[46] Pricing policy was central to this review: both for domestic sales and for exports, price was to be the factor determining sales volume, and not the other way around. This price was to reflect real market value, and thus fall in line with the 'international correlation between energy volumes and the prices of the various energy sources'.[47] This in fact came down to Dutch natural gas following pertinent oil products prices as determined primarily by the crude oil pricing and volume policies pursued by the OPEC countries. In the opinion of the Minister, such a pricing policy for Dutch natural gas was not only in itself required in the present circumstances in order to responsibly safeguard long-term natural gas supply, but was also a prerequisite for the continuing exploration and production of new sources and deposits. The negotiations conducted by Mr Spierenburg had as a result that, by 1982, export prices to a large extent met with the Minister's objectives. Negotiations, from then on again conducted by Gasunie itself, finally achieved these objectives by the end of 1984.[48] As this Dutch natural gas pricing policy was followed by Norway and the Soviet Union, this meant that from 1985, full linkage to competing oil products had become the basis of all price-formation for natural gas in continental Western Europe, with the exception of Algerian gas.

The simultaneous announcement by the Minister that the export limitation instituted in 1974 – namely that no new volumes beyond those already contractually agreed at the time were to be made available for exportation – was to be lifted was wholly in accord with this policy conception. But not without conditions attached: the Minister explicitly added that in appraising new export obligations he would, on the basis of his authority to allow or disallow them, employ as prime criteria price, date of delivery and scope of obligations. Price was to be considered in the light of the international market, and a premium would have to be paid for load-factor flexibility, while the other two criteria were almost wholly to be determined by the technical possibilities and the gas reserves situation. This policy, in the Minister's view, was in accordance with parallel international interests.[49] This

---

[46] Kamerstukken II 1983/84, nr. 18100, hoofdstuk XIII, pp. 101 *ff*.
[47] Ibidem, p. 109.
[48] *Gasunie 1984 Annual Report*, p. 22.
[49] Kamerstukken referred to in footnote 46, p. 114.

lifting of the export limitation resulted in Gasunie's being able to agree with its foreign customers for an extension of export deliveries after expiry of the current contract period, meaning that between 1995 and 2010 around 280×10^9 m^3 of Dutch gas will still be exported. Because of this the tailing-off of Dutch exports, which was contractually to begin in 1994 and was to run to 2000, will be moved forward in time to the period from 2004–2010, while export volume will be maintained at about 27×10^9 m^3 per year between 1994 and 2004. Including these additional exports, recoverable Dutch natural gas reserves, according to present predictions, will have dropped to a level of between 426 and 586 $\times 10^9$ m^3 around the year 2010.[50]

For the Community's long-term natural gas supply, as it had to be judged on the basis of existing prospects at the beginning of 1983, a critical period was to begin after 1995 in which a potential supply surplus would suddenly turn into a substantial demand surplus. For not only would Dutch export contracts (not yet renewed at that time) then be in their tailing-off phase, but the Norwegian Ekofisk contracts too would begin their tail-off around 1995, terminating altogether in 1997/98. Moreover, in 2000, about half of the contracted imports of natural gas from the Soviet Union to the Community were – and still are – to be phased out, and in that same year a considerable part of the contracted imports from Algeria was also – and also still is – to be phased out. Because lead-times for the development of potentially available new major production projects have to be put at some seven to ten years, the predictable shortfall after 1995 was in fact already acute in the mid-Eighties.[51] Both in political circles and in the gas companies, attention focussed on the natural gas deposit discovered on the Norwegian continental shelf in 1979, which was later to become known as the Troll field. The proven reserves of this field had been determined at $1,200 \times 10^9$ m^3, thus making it the largest natural gas deposit in Western Europe after the Groningen gas field. However, sea depth on location is 300–340 meters, and in view of the enormous investments required for the development of this project, it was clear from the outset that production could only be profitable in the presence of a sales market sufficiently willing and able to support this. For Norway herself there was no compelling reason to arrive at a short-term decision to bring the Troll field into production; Norway would after all be able to generate sufficient revenue from the further development of her oil production. So the response had to come from the European sales market. In 1984 the purchasing consortium consisting mainly of Ruhrgas, Gasunie, Gaz de France and Distrigaz began negotiations with the Norwegian state enterprise Statoil. In July 1986, an

[50] Gasunie 1987 Gas Marketing Plan.
[51] COM (84) 120 final of 13 April 1984, p. 13.
   COM (84) 583 final of 26 October 1984, p. 7.

138

agreement was reached on the basis of an oil products price parity formula which in essence was the same as that which had in the meantime been established for export deliveries of Dutch gas. It may be argued without exaggeration that if the Netherlands had not in 1985 finally achieved complete linkage with competing oil products prices and also contractually secured it for her extended export deliveries to 2010, the Community gas market would probably have offered the Norwegian Government insufficient reliable long-term prospects to approve the agreement reached on the Troll gas. The alternative would then have been to start urgent negotiations primarily with the Soviet Union for the delivery of considerable additional amounts of natural gas in order to adequately safeguard natural gas supply for Western Europe after 1995. As has already been indicated, this alternative was not at all attractive on political grounds.[52] Was this what Minister van Aardenne was thinking of when he concluded in 1983 that his new export policy was in accordance with parallel international interests?

The agreements reached in 1986 for Troll gas also comprise the delivery, based on the same price formula, of natural gas from the Sleipner field, which is much smaller and lies further to the south. Initially, Sleipner gas had been the subject of a purchasing agreement between the British Gas Corporation and Statoil, but this agreement did not in the end receive British Government approval, because it was felt that the price was too high and that for the time being, British gas reserves in the North Sea were sufficient to guaranteeing domestic gas supply to the end of the century.[53] Thus the United Kingdom persisted in its isolation. The importance of the Sleipner field for the continental Western European market derives from the fact that, because this field can be brought into production more rapidly, deliveries of the new Norwegian gas will be able to start as early as 1993.[54] Production from the Troll field will be able to start in 1995 at the earliest. As from 2002, total delivery will amount to about 20×10^9 m^3 per year and remain at that level for twenty years. One half of this will be transported to Emden via the Ekofisk Centre, the other half will be conveyed to Zeebrugge via a 1,100 km pipeline to be newly built. In Emden and Zeebrugge there will be connections to the European network of main transport lines. Contracted amounts for the period 1993 – 2022 run to 450×10^9 m^3. Besides this, the contracts provide for optional quantities amounting to 360×10^9 m^3. At the end of 1986, the Austrian company OMV AG contracted to buy an amount of 1×10^9 m^3 per year for a period of 20 years. This means that at this moment only about 40% (some 500×10^9 m^3) of reserves considered recoverable from the fields concerned are available for sale.

[52] COM (86) 518 final of 11 December 1986, pp. 3, 12. See also A. Giraud and X. Boy de la Tour, op. cit., p. 395.
[53] *Oil & Gas Journal*, February 18, 1985 pp. 68, 69.
[54] *Gasunie 1986 Annual Report*, pp. 13, 14.

5. Conclusion

The current and the future European natural gas market can be best explained with the aid of *Figure 2* which shows natural gas supply for the continental Western European market as it has presently been contractually agreed upon with the various producers (volumes converted to Groningen quality). The lowest supply volume in this diagram comprises Dutch exports including the latest contract revisions. The supply volume indicated above this represents domestic demand covered by domestic production. (Note: Not included in the figure are the domestic productions in West Germany, Italy, France and Denmark. For 1990, they together will amount to about 37×10^9 m^3, and thereafter follow more or less the same pattern as the domestic production in the Netherlands.) The three highest volumes respectively reflect contracted imports of natural gas from the Soviet Union, Norway and Algeria. The Norwegian volume includes quantities contracted from the Troll and Sleipner fields. The diagram indicates that until 2000, supply and demand will be reasonably balanced. After this, supply drops very abruptly in relation to demand. The demand curve reflects growth rates of 1.5% to 1990 and 1.1% for the years beyond. Supply volume comprises a certain upward flexibility, but because total volume is fixed, a higher rate of gas offtake would entail a shift to the left of the falling supply curves indicated in the diagram for the period after 2000. This would mean that substantial supplementary quantities would have to reach the Western European market as early as between 1995 and 2000. Whether this will be possible is a difficult question to answer. In any case, after 2000 a major proportion of the new quantities will have to come from natural gas deposits which have barely been discovered yet and whose extent and recoverability are by no means yet certain. For instance, as far as Norway is concerned, one must think of the recent discovery of natural gas reservoirs offshore Hammerfest, and the exploration of the Barentssea, which hardly has started.

For the post-2000 gas supply, technological and financial commitments that are virtually unimaginable, by present-day standards, will be required to undertake exploration and production and the transport of the natural gas from the production locations to the sales markets in the Community. Moreover, the Community gas market will have to generate enough economic incentives for those commitments to be actually made. The foundations for this are already there: a reasonably coherent Community gas market (in which hopefully the United Kingdom will be able to participate before 2000) based on the cornerstones discussed in the course of this study. The Community's energy policy must remain oriented towards creating conditions in which gas companies can co-operate with one another to extend and strengthen these foundations. The infrastructural provisions for the Community gas market are still a long way from completion and will continue to require major investments. Spain has already expressed its desire to be connected to

140

the European network of main transport lines by means of a new North-South system fed by Norwegian gas via Zeebrugge through Belgium and France and by Algerian gas to be landed in Spain in the form of LNG or via a pipeline to be constructed across the Mediterranean. There will have to be further extensions of the flexibility of the intra-Community supply system and the stand-by facilities between gas companies in order to safeguard gas supply. In addition, at the level of the consumers, the natural gas market will have to be further improved qualitatively by increasing the actual efficiency of natural gas as an energy source and by expanding the possibilities for high-grade applications of natural gas, both in industry and the household. This means that in the downstream sector considerable effort will likewise be required in order to enable the Community to assure itself of natural gas as an important factor in its primary energy supply after 2000. More than has been the case up till now, the Community will have to orient its policy regarding gas supply towards long-term developments in the international energy market, and formulate Community objectives accordingly. In other words: the Community will have to create the conditions to be able to maintain a striking balance between the differing demands of 'consumers' logic' and 'producers' logic'.

Figure 1

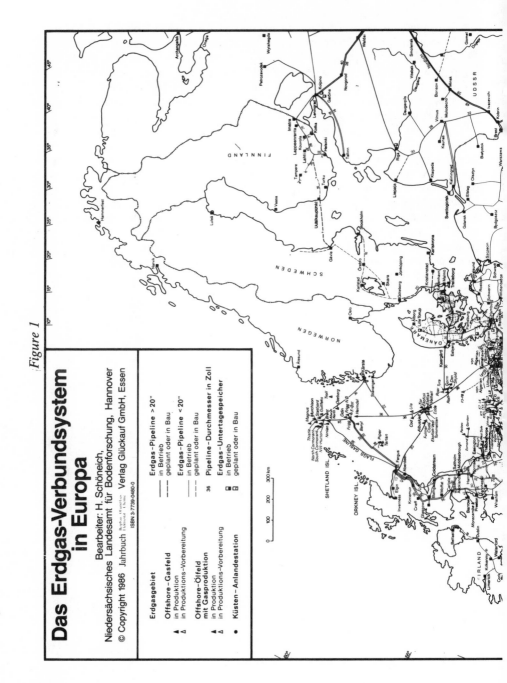

142

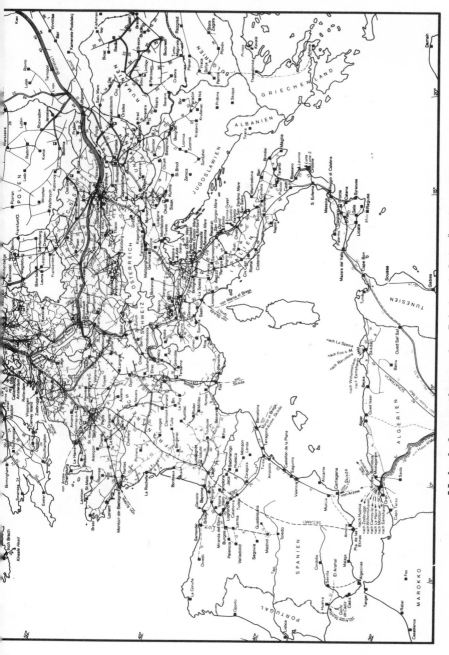

Mehr Informationen im Jahrbuch 86/87 Bergbau · Öl und Gas
Elektrizität · Chemie

143

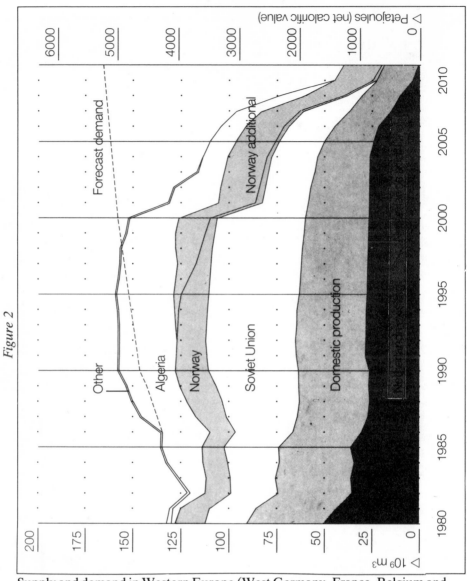

Figure 2

Supply and demand in Western Europe (West Germany, France, Belgium and Italy) in billion m³.

The agreed extension of the Dutch contracts and the additional purchases from the Norwegian Troll field mean that supplies on the West European gas market are assured until into next century.

144